THE REAL CLASSROOM

TALES AND LESSONS FROM SCHOOL

JIM SACK

STONE MOOSE PUBLISHING

CONTENTS

SPRING

SUMMER

Eileen and I have been married for thirty-seven years as I write this and we're still happy, in love, and best friends. Our children, Adam, Joshua, and Emily, are the perfect result of our marriage and I expect to stay close with them as the years continue to fly by. I dedicate this book to my family.

ACKNOWLEDGMENTS

I wanted to be a veterinarian until my next door neighbor, John Mizerak, took me on a visit to Cornell University. Dogs with cancerous tumors to be used by those in the veterinary science program, as well as the grasshopper experiment (a story for another day) were signs that I would never be a vet.

While tobogganing with friends, the sled flipped over and the person in front of me rolled over my ankle, breaking it. Although Jeff and Buzzy were there to make a splint for my leg, it was Amy Cohen who broke it in the first place. For obvious reasons I never thanked her, but that event led me indirectly to teaching because....

While on crutches I assisted a professor with statistics work at a nearby elementary school and then began volunteering there. Kingsborough Elementary School was the first "open school" I had ever seen and where I thought about becoming a teacher for the first time.

I worked in four school districts as either a teacher or principal and was fortunate to have had many wonderful colleagues, certainly too numerous to mention by name. Thanks to you all!

After having spent thirty years teaching children, I can honestly say that there was not one single day when I didn't look forward to seeing my students. I'm still in contact with quite a few through social media, and then there's the occasional breakfast or lunch together. Kids (and animals) are the best!

For forty-five years, Paul and Dottie Rabin have been a part of my life. When our kids were younger, they'd always ask for a Paul and Dottie story, of which there are many. If you see me in the near future, I'll share a couple. Thanks Paul, Dottie, Bonnie, and Kim!

I want to offer my sincerest thanks to all those who contributed to *The Real Classroom*. Many of the stories, quotes, and yes, the pet peeves, were shared with me from their experiences as teachers, parents, and as children. Much appreciated!

Jim

PREFACE

In my backyard were two ceramic chickens. They were "given" to me by neighbors after I spent a school day in a chicken costume walking around clucking and flapping my "wings" for students as a reading reward. I'm sure I looked pretty silly, but, then again, there was that time I wore a tutu and a big hoop skirt...

"What time did you get home today, 2:00? It must be nice to work five hours a day."
"Another vacation? Didn't you just have one? And then you have summer off, too?"

These are the kind of comments my brother often made. It's ok, though, because he's a lawyer and we all know that lawyers play golf every day and charge too much.

INTRODUCTION

My fifth grade class had earned their very first pizza party, although I don't remember what for. The kids all sat there with their plates, ready to enjoy the large pizza that had just been delivered to our classroom. One of my students volunteered to pass out the slices, took about three steps, and then dropped the entire pizza face-down on our carpeted floor! That was the first and only time that I ever had a student pass out pizza or any main dish to be shared instead of having each student come up individually. Fool me once.

The Real Classroom: Tales And Lessons From School grew out of the idea that you can't make this stuff up, and from the many times teachers like myself stated, "I ought to write a book". It's also a chance to share what I've learned over the years because I was an educator and you'd think I'd have learned a few things.

For example, I learned long ago that everyone thinks they understand teaching and learning because they went to school when they were growing up. Unlike most professions, just about everyone had daily contact with teachers. Teachers gave homework and punished the bad kids, corrected papers and taught us stuff that we might need to know, and had meetings with parents and other teachers. Pretty basic stuff... but not really.

There are a few ground rules as you read this book.

- Many of these "classroom tales" are from my own experiences as a teacher and principal, but quite a few others were shared by colleagues and friends.
- For the sake of confidentiality, no real names are used and if there is a "Mr. R.", for example, chances are that I changed the initial and/or the person's gender.
- You will see a quote or an occasional pet peeve shared at the beginning of each chapter. Although some are related to the chapter topic, many are not, but were included because I found them to be funny, sad, or just interesting.

Finally, if you have a moment, please consider writing a short review of *The Real Classroom* on your favorite book selling website- I'd appreciate it!

FALL

1

SETTING UP YOUR CLASSROOM

"Everything's different now that you're gone. I'm not weird anymore. I tried, but so far I just can't be funny. I guess when you left you took the weirdness out of me."

S etting up my classroom was one of the great joys of teaching for me. I'd usually spend at least parts of eight to ten summer days coming into school to set up my classroom and that's when the fun began. Unlike most professions, teachers get to start fresh every year both with a new class and with a classroom set up any way they wanted. There were numerous patterns for student desks and multiple options for arranging and storing art supplies, bookcases, your teacher desk, etc. In addition, the arrangement can be changed anytime you like. I probably rearranged the student desks in my room six to eight different ways during the typical school year and made numerous changes to bulletin boards, placement of classroom furniture, etc. Part of this was based on the changing needs of my students and part was due to my being restless.

Classroom Tales...

I still remember the day I set up my classroom for the first time. I wanted a physical environment that would encourage a sense of unity and focus. We would all get to know each other, but I still wanted my students to be facing me at the front of the room. I decided on a "fan shape" that would spread out the farther back in the class you went. I set up the desks, but then shifted each desk a few inches, and repeated this process at least 3 times before it was perfect. On the first day of school, it probably took about thirty-five seconds before desks were moved around and out of that perfect shape I had created. Lesson learned.

I was in school moving books around on a very large bookcase when the wheels in front fell off. I held up the front of the bookcase so it wouldn't fall on me while the books continued sliding off hitting me.

My partner was the world's best decorator, but in order to keep things in great shape she laminated everything and couldn't figure out why everyone was mad at her. I explained that she was wiping out the laminator supplies for the entire school.

One summer weekend I was using a step stool to put up decorations. I was on the top step (the one that says "don't stand on this step") when the stool collapsed. I dropped like a rock (think Coyote in the Road Runner cartoons) and hit the floor. Stunned, I lay there for a moment or two thinking that if I couldn't move, I wouldn't be found until Monday.

I was teaching in an open school where classroom space was defined by bookshelves, bulletin boards, etc.. One teacher moved these items so her area was bigger than the classroom next to her. The principal directed her to move these items back or else he would have it done after hours. She wouldn't, so he did.

After my principal promised me that I wouldn't have to change rooms for quite a while, I painted the outlines for maps of the USA and the world and had my students finish the work during the first week. They looked beautiful! At the end of that year, I found out I'd be moving to a different room. The teacher who moved into that room the following year said that her class appreciated our work.

...and Lessons Learned

If you're a bit of a neat freak like me, you're in for a rude awakening. Student desks will never be in the same place at the end of the day. The same thing goes for books, art supplies, etc.

Posters and other finished products from educational supply companies are nice and add color to your classroom, but displaying student work is extremely important. Kids love to see their best work posted and it serves to motivate them.

How you set up your student desks really determines how you will teach and how your students will learn. I was usually not a "rows" guy and often had students working together in pairs or groups, so my desks were often in "clusters" of 3-5 desks. Sometimes, though, the needs of a particular class suggested a different grouping, including having all desks facing front.

I almost always started out the school year with my student desks in a big "U" shape, with the remaining desks facing each other inside the

"U". They had a few days to get used to their classmates and I had a few days to figure out seating combinations that would work.

Keep some basic tools in your desk for those occasions when desk or table legs need to be tightened, or you need to fix a broken pencil sharpener. I always had an allen wrench, a screw driver, needle nose pliers, etc. By the way, a broom and dustpan came in handy more times than I care to remember, and I could've made a fortune if I charged other teachers when those items were borrowed.

Decide how open you want to be with your students regarding your personal life. Many teachers display family photos and personal items in their classroom, but I worked with teachers that wanted to maintain a pretty strong divide between home and work. Whatever way works best for you!

2

THE FIRST DAY OF SCHOOL FOR ADULTS

"You've made us laugh so many times (but we know not to laugh when you get serious)."

Teachers want to be treated as professionals, both in stature and salary. This makes absolute sense to me because I've always believed that teaching young children shapes our nation for generations to come and, therefore, is as important a profession as any other. Teachers, as professionals, also want to be prepared for this important position by having their classrooms set up effectively, having a clear understanding of the materials they will be using in instruction, completing any training necessary in regards to new materials, school procedures, etc. and, finally, having all schedules and coordination of programming for students up and running- all before the students begin arriving for their new school year. Certainly, administrators want this also, as do school board members and parents. The question then becomes, how prepared are teachers for the start of the school year?

Classroom Tales...

At one point in the summer, letters arrived in the mail from my school district. They contained the usual information, hoping I had a good summer, sharing all of the work that had been done at school during the vacation, and welcoming me back. Then, I would read the schedule and see that my day or days before students arrived would be taken up with meetings and speeches. Yikes!

One year on the first day of school for faculty members we had a speaker. She happened to stand right next to me as she was speaking- as in less than two feet away- and stayed there the entire time, even putting her hand on my shoulder occasionally to emphasize a point. I have no idea what she spoke about, but I do know it was one of the most uncomfortable meetings I've ever had.

My first year as a principal, I held my first faculty meeting. I welcomed new staff members and asked if anyone had any news they wanted to share. At that time, a teacher stood up and began shouting at the Union reps about the terrible conditions in the building.

My first day as a new teacher was wonderful because the administrators made sure there was plenty of time for teachers to work in their rooms. The best part of the day was when students from kindergarten through twelfth grade spoke to the entire district faculty on what they liked about school and what could be better. Afterwards, I asked the seventh grader who acted as the "emcee" who her teacher would be in my subject area and it turned out it was me!

I always over planned for the first day. I actually had plans for the week on that day just because I didn't want the kids to be bored.

. . .

One year I "looped" with my students who I had been with in fourth grade which meant that we could just start right in. They came in "high-fiving" everyone and it was great because they were a really good class. It also meant that they couldn't say "we didn't do that last year".

...and Lessons Learned

Administrators seem to always fill the day or days before kids arrive with meetings, introductions of new staff, and welcome back speeches. Although some of this may be warranted, teachers generally have one thing on their minds and that is the need to work in their classrooms.

Motivational speakers, especially, should never be scheduled at the beginning of the school year. Teachers who are negative at the start of the school year probably aren't going to change. Teachers who have a more positive attitude don't need the "rah rah" speech then, and all teachers want to work in their rooms and do other practical things to get ready for kids. If you want to have a motivational speaker, have them visit in January, or better yet, March.

3

THE FIRST DAY OF SCHOOL WITH KIDS

One student to another walking down the hall with their teacher. "Don't talk. She has eyes in the back of her head and can see you."

Many of us have an image of what the first day is like. Mom and/or Dad are out at the bus stop wondering how their kids got to be so old, possibly taking pictures or a video as their child heads off or gets on the bus. Tears sometimes flow, especially for that new kindergartener. Students getting on a bus choose where to sit, unless seats are assigned, and then hear about bus rules- the first occurrence in a long line of adults sharing rules with kids that day.

Once at school, kids walk through the halls to their new classroom, while the adults in school maintain happy faces as they guide, point, or explain to children where they have to go. In some cases, an adult will take a child or two by the hand and deliver them themselves. A lot of elementary schools send some kind of tag with a color or animal shape and maybe a teacher's name so kids get to the correct classroom. Once inside their classroom, other than friends they were in contact with over the summer, kids look around to see who else they know while the teacher welcomes students and guides them to where to put their supplies and to their new desk.

Classroom Tales...

As a teacher, my first day with students actually began the night before. I never slept well, even after teaching for fifteen or twenty years, probably from the excitement and anticipation of meeting my new class the next day. I always dreamed that I wasn't in my classroom when my new students arrived- not a good way to start the school year. Sometimes the dream included car trouble, sometimes I got delayed in the hall, or sometimes I was talking to another teacher.

We played the "Name Game" to get the kids out of their seats. I wrote the names of famous people, animals, or characters on index cards, one for each kid, and attached a card to each student's back. Then, everyone walked around the classroom asking "yes or no" questions to classmates until they guessed what the name was. It worked well except once in a while, when a student didn't know a name or couldn't read the name, like Mickey Mouse.

I was the new teacher in the building and was really nervous since this was my first teaching job. I didn't sleep well the night before the kids' first day, but the day was going well. Reading was great and math was excellent. We then got up to go to gym and everyone got in line. I had a line leader and the kids were in the order I set up and then...Oh my gosh, I realized I didn't know where the gym was.

I taped a homework pass to the bottom of a desk before students arrived. They got really excited to find out who had won the pass when I mentioned it during the day.

. . .

The first homework assignment I gave was actually for my students' parents. It was called Memory Lane and it asked parents to share what they remembered about being in third grade (or a similar grade). Many wrote about their friends, favorite lunch in the cafeteria, a teacher, or a project they did. The kids loved having their parents assigned homework and it reminded parents what it was like to be in elementary school. I posted these on the wall outside my classroom before Meet The Teacher Night. One year, two parents who hadn't seen each other since they were in third grade saw the names and reconnected. Pretty cool.

My first year as principal I was outside welcoming students as they got off the buses and walked back into my school excited for the first full day. My excitement turned to shock when I walked in and saw several hundred children standing or sitting in the lobby. It seems that the teacher's contractual day started ten minutes after kids began arriving so students were not allowed to go to their classrooms.

By the end of the first day, students and teachers were tired. Summer vacation was over and all that was left to do was to go home, tell friends and family about your new class, and figure out what you were going to wear the next day. After all, there are only so many new shirts or pairs of pants you have.

...and Lessons Learned

Depending on your experience level and self confidence, this is the day when you set the tone for your class. It's not just about handing out books and going over rules- it's about establishing the framework for the kind of class you want to have. Your kids usually will be feeling a mix of excitement and nervousness, so this first day is when they are most "pliable". Take advantage of it!

. . .

Take your new class on a "tour" of the school. It gives you a chance to establish hallway expectations, show students where the bathrooms, cafeteria, gym, etc. are and gets everyone out of their seats for a while. This is especially important for any kids new to the school, but it's really effective for everyone because teachers change rooms, new teachers are hired, and quite a few students are likely to attend speech, OT/PT, etc. This way, they start to get a feel for the different places in school they would be going.

The number one topic on the minds of many kids is the bathroom. They want to know when they can go and whether there is a tag, a sign out sheet, etc. In other words, what are the bathroom rules? By the way, students new to the school also want to know <u>where</u> it is. Remember the tour?

The number two topic is homework, depending on the grade. My third graders always wanted to know how often they would have homework, how much they would have, and how hard it was going to be.

I never assigned seats the first day of school. I did this for two reasons. First, kids are usually nervous the first day so I let them sit where they want. Second, I didn't really know them at that point so I took three to five days to get a feel for who got along, which kids could work together, and what each of their personalities was like.

I was always big on my students earning responsibilities and privileges. I had a Garfield poster on the wall that said, "Privileges: Abuse 'Em And You'll Lose 'Em", and I referred to it often. My students knew that their behavior, attitude, and work habits dictated the kind of class we were going to have.

. . .

Just like touring the school, take the kids on a "tour of the room". It may seem silly, but I wanted my students to know where everything was, like art supplies, paper, baskets for turning in homework and notes from home. It was also important that they know what things were off limits to them, such as my desk, unless they had permission to go in it.

4

THE PLEDGE OF ALLEGIANCE

"I learned many things from you like how to be respectful and responsible. You also have taught me that learning can be fun."

I grew up saying the Pledge of Allegiance in school each and every day. It was a tradition, part of our morning routine, sometimes led by a student or adult over the public address system so the entire school could say it together, and other times led by a student or teacher in the classroom. It was a sign of patriotism, of recognizing those who fought for our freedom, and a way to show that we were loyal Americans. I don't think many of us gave it a lot of thought- at least I didn't- and I'm not sure how many kids understood what the words meant. We just stood each morning, placed our right hand (if we knew which was the right hand) over our hearts (at least in the general area of our hearts) and repeated the words as best we could.

Classroom Tales...

Two of my new fifth graders were Jehovah's Witnesses and, although I'm far from being an expert, I believe pledging allegiance to an object, such as a flag, is not allowed. These students stood out of respect, but didn't recite the pledge.

We said the Pledge every day in my class in every year that I was teaching, along with the rest of our school. One of the boys decided to show off by going really fast and speaking in an especially loud voice. I gave him my "teacher face", the one that all teachers have.

Kids in every class took turns leading the school in the Pledge over the PA system. In fifth grade, we had to go really slow when the younger kids had their turn, but kids in all grades mispronounced lots of words.

One boy wanted attention more than he cared about my "teacher face". I asked him if he needed to practice the Pledge at recess, but he didn't seem to care. Then I suggested that the entire class needed to participate so he could "model" the correct way. His classmates weren't happy with him at all! Peer pressure works.

I was subbing at a school where the Pledge and morning announcements were shown live on video throughout the school. I thought it was great, but the students who sit in front of the camera should probably be reminded that the entire school can see them for the five to ten minutes they're on camera before they actually begin.

...and Lessons Learned

I remember beginning the year with a social studies unit on America-things like the Constitution, the Bill of Rights, etc. Kids earned points for tasks completed, one of which was to recite the Pledge of Allegiance aloud to me and then explain what some of the words meant, such as "pledge" and "indivisible". Students are more likely to respect the Pledge when they know what it means.

When reciting the Pledge, it takes occasional reminders to students about respecting our country and those who have fought for our freedom. I always tied the three things together, the flag, the Pledge, and those who've sacrificed to keep us free- students relate to people easier than to a pledge or a flag.

5

BREAKFAST IN SCHOOL

"My friend in your class tells me that your hair is not as dark as it was
when I had you as a teacher."

Most school districts I'm familiar with serve breakfast in school, the theory being that children are much more likely to succeed in school if they start off the day with a healthy breakfast, which they may not get at home. It makes sense, so offering breakfast in school really shouldn't be an issue, should it? Still, like many school issues, there are other factors to consider, such as staffing if the cafeteria is used, what students who aren't eating breakfast are doing at this time, etc. Finally, the biggest question is whether schools should be responsible for providing breakfast at all, a responsibility that has historically been a part of parenting.

Classroom Tales...

I remember having students eating breakfast in the cafeteria and staying there as long as possible so they wouldn't have to start their work. Luckily, those who were supervising in the cafeteria would keep an eye on them and the clock and "move them along".

I had one girl who would often come down to the room and start the day with us before remembering that she hadn't eaten breakfast yet. She would rush down to the cafeteria to eat, which meant that she would be behind when she returned or that she had to bring her breakfast back with her because the people supervising breakfast had other places to be.

As a Resource Room teacher, it can be a problem. I'm supposed to see kids in a group at 8:30 and they're often late because they're eating breakfast. I have to go down and remind them to eat quickly. It's not fun for them or me.

...and Lessons Learned

This will sound cold, and not what most people who know me would expect, but I wish that schools would stop providing breakfast. It's not the job of schools to do this and it causes many problems in terms of scheduling, space needs, and financial issues, as well as allowing parents to avoid this responsibility. I understand and agree that kids should start the day with breakfast. I also understand the changes in family structure in society and the financial challenges families face, but that is not the fault of school personnel and the solution is not to dump this responsibility on schools. It encourages the view that schools provide child care services. Schools exist to educate.

Assuming your school continues, or begins, offering breakfast, you must have a process that ensures that students who participate do not miss academic time in the classroom. Learning must remain the top priority for students. When planning the time frame for breakfast, the location, staffing, etc., students who get breakfast in school must be ready for their academic day when it begins.

6

HOME SCHOOL COMMUNICATION

After explaining the activities to a kindergarten class, the PE teacher asks if there are any questions. Responses include "You're the best gym teacher ever!", "I like your hair", and "You're very pretty."

S ometimes on Facebook someone will share one of those "back in the day" posts about what school was like when they were growing up. Included might be a comment about the trouble you'd get into if a teacher called home or wrote a note about something you did or didn't do in school. After all, a teacher's word was law when it came to school.

The day to day communication between home and school seems quite different now than in previous decades. Parents and teachers still write notes or make phone calls, but also rely on newer technologies. In districts I'm familiar with, not only are homework assignments and reminders written in a notebook or agenda, they may also be explained on a teacher's webpage. A teacher needs to know who the child was with the night before or where he/she is going after school, which may involve a babysitter, an after school program, more than one home because of a split family or work hours, a grand-parent, etc.

Classroom Tales...

Later in my teaching career, I gave my phone number to my students and their parents and encouraged them to call with any questions or concerns. Most families never called, but I did hear from some about specific assignments, field trips, etc. Some students called quite often about homework or just to talk, and one used to sing Christmas carols to me over the phone.

As a principal in a new district, I was appalled when I realized that the only school phone teachers could use to call their student's homes was on the counter in the main office.

One of the most embarrassing occurrences was when I would call a student's home to speak with a parent and I used the wrong last name. Between divorces, boyfriends or girlfriends, grandparents, etc. it was hard to keep track of who the adults were in the home.

...and Lessons Learned

Contact parents as often as possible in several ways. I'm a talker, so I called parents on the phone. Email, notes, video chats, etc. are all viable options, but base your choice on what's most convenient for parents, as well as realistic for you as a teacher.

Share good news as often as possible and always begin any communication with positive comments. Historically, a call or note from the teacher was never welcomed as it was expected to be bad news. It's very important that parents see communication between home and school as a good thing.

Home school communication is a two way street. Encourage parents to contact you with questions or concerns, or just to talk or check in. This may not be your favorite part of the job, but it's important.

Chances are you'll have students who have step parents or whose parents are separated or divorced. If that's the case, unless there are specific or legal reasons not to do so, maintain good communications with both parents, or with whatever adults are involved in raising your students.

The other side to what I wrote above is when parents who are no longer together both expect to be informed of their child's progress, not just occasionally, but on an almost daily basis. That may mean that each wants copies of the day's homework assignments, and every note and letter regarding class projects, parties, field trips, and school functions. That may not be realistic.

7

READ ALOUD TO KIDS

"Whenever I watch or read Harry Potter, I'll think of you."

As a classroom teacher, I read aloud a different book each month strictly for pleasure- there was no curriculum connection, necessarily, because my reading aloud to my students was for fun. Truthfully, I hoped it would encourage my students to enjoy reading more, and because there was such variety in the books I read, I felt there was something for everyone.

My September book was "The Twits", by Roald Dahl, which was the story of a rather disgusting couple named Mr. and Mrs. Twit. It was gross, just enough to make everyone comfortable as they settled into a new grade. My October selection was "The Monster's Ring", by Bruce Coville. It was the perfect story for October because it was a little scary, a little creepy, and had a surprise ending. If my timing was good, I finished it on Halloween! Then, it was on to the next month's selection.

Classroom Tales …

My December book was "The Best Christmas Pageant Ever", by Barbara Robinson. It was about a local Christmas pageant that starred the worst kids in town, the Herdmans. We had lots of discussions about Jesus, the Holy Spirit, and the Three Wise Men- not typical topics in a public school, especially with a teacher who grew up in a Jewish home.

Sometimes, the choices for books didn't work out. One book about a dog who lost his sight and the young girl who took care of him seemed to go on forever and the kids developed that "glazed" look that told me they found it boring. I also read a book that had occasional words that were not quite appropriate for 3rd grade- I just changed a word here and there if I needed to, but I walked back into my room one day from a meeting just in time to hear the person covering my class utter a word from the book that should have been bleeped out. Students perked right up!

My favorite read aloud books were the "Bunnicula" books by James Howe. There were 3 of them, I think, and one character was a dachshund named Howie. I was laughing so hard at one point that I was actually crying, and the kids were looking at me wondering what was going on.

I arranged for my third graders to take turns reading to a preschool class and most loved it. That day's reader would have to get an appropriate book from the library and practice reading it aloud before going to see the younger kids. Some of my students who did this weren't really great readers, but the younger kids enjoyed the visits anyway.

· · ·

I usually read to my students when I sat in my rocking chair and they sat on the floor in front of me. One year, I would put on these fun shoes that had hair on them, almost like fur, and one girl liked to pet the fur while I was reading.

...and Lessons Learned

It's so difficult to find time for everything you feel you need to get done as a classroom teacher. There is so much material to get through and then the fire alarm goes off, there's an assembly, or a group of students leaves for extra help in a subject. Reading aloud to children is so important, though, that it has to be a priority, even for ten minutes a day. Find a way to make it happen.

Not every teacher is comfortable or even talented when it comes to reading aloud with enthusiasm and the proper inflection for a book's characters. Try your best, though!

There are many students who are fabulous when it comes to reading aloud. Make arrangements with a teacher in a lower grade for your students to read aloud to the kids in that class. The younger kids will love having a "big kid" read to them and your student gets great experience and a boost to their ego at the same time.

Choose your read alouds carefully. Your choices may include books tied in to your curriculum, while others may just be for fun. I tried to find out what books were read aloud in previous grades and avoided them and also spoke with teachers in the next grade or two- after all, even if you have favorites that you enjoy reading to kids, if they've heard it before, they may not enjoy it again. This is tougher than it sounds because, although there are many wonderful books to choose from, there is still a pretty good chance that the book you choose may have been read by one or more of your students. Still, all of those good books!

If possible, set up a part of your room for reading aloud. If you're an elementary teacher, your students just don't take up that much space (unless you have a huge class) so an area rug or carpet squares should work nicely. I suppose there's nothing wrong with reading to kids while they sit at their desks, but I always found it a little too formal.

8

HOMEWORK

"I'm so happy that I got to have you as a teacher."

Homework is one aspect of school that seems to have undergone a transformation over the years. When kids were growing up a few decades ago, time spent on homework competed only with time spent playing with friends indoors or outdoors. There were not that many organized activities, and those that were offered seemed to take place on the weekends or the occasional weeknight. In this day and age, kids are often scheduled for different sports and hobbies throughout the week, with homework sometimes taking a back seat. The image of a child sitting at the kitchen table while doing homework, getting help when needed, and then having it checked by mom or dad, while not uncommon, isn't the norm for many families. One aspect of homework that has not changed too much are the excuses used by students who haven't completed the assignments. The homework was lost, forgotten, and even eaten by... you know.

Classroom Tales...

My favorite excuse given by students over the years was that they didn't have time to finish their homework. I would ask what time they got home, what time they ate dinner, etc. and, almost without fail, there were big gaps in time when the homework could have been completed.

One student brought in a note from a parent that explained why that night's homework wasn't done. I accepted that excuse...once.

A parent called me after the first few weeks of school because she was concerned about her child doing homework for two to three hours a night. It seems that he took my message about always turning in your best work seriously and was redoing every assignment until it was perfect.

One student brought in homework clearly in an adult's handwriting and he swore up and down that he wrote it. Even when we brought it up at parent conferences it continued. What was really sad is that many of the answers were wrong.

"It's called "H O M E work" because it's supposed to be done at home." It was my standard response when kids tried to rush through it during the school day, or admitted it was done on the bus or in the car.

Our son, who struggled with school work in general, just sat on the floor one night and screamed "I can't do this!" while attempting to do his homework. As teachers, this made us rethink about how some of our students might be reacting to homework we had assigned.

I was teaching when a colleague came over to explain that my son, who was a student in one of the other classes in my grade level, had turned in homework in pen, rather than the required pencil, because "there were no pencils in my house".

...and Lessons Learned

If at all possible, don't give homework on the first day of school. Let your students breathe and, besides, they have enough new stuff to digest that first day.

For quite a few years, I gave homework every night. Then, as more and more students came from broken homes, I began trying, not always successfully, to avoid assigning homework on Fridays. Kids had different rules with different parents and would sometimes leave class materials at the "part time" home. I'm not suggesting that teachers not assign homework on weekends, but at least try to understand the life students go home to.

Every so often I'd get a note from a parent who tried to help their child with last night's homework, but couldn't. Even young parents have forgotten how to do some of the things in their kid's homework assignments and even if they knew how to do the assignment, they may have learned different strategies than their child's teacher is using. A lot of parents don't remember how to multiply fractions and they might not know much about the rivers in Europe.

. . .

Speaking of understanding, put yourself in your students' shoes and give them "the night off" when there is a school concert, Halloween, etc. Let them know that you're choosing to give them the night off and they'll appreciate it. It also gives you "chips" to cash in at a later date. In other words, I let my students know that there's a trade off.

Having a good working relationship with parents means you'll be aware of homework problems quickly. If a student goes day after day without homework or is taking 2-3 hours to complete their homework each night, a parent who's comfortable with their child's teacher will contact the teacher with their concern.

Homework should have a purpose and should be reviewed or graded each day. Kids quickly learn whether their homework is going to matter and react accordingly.

When I was teaching, recess was considered something that my students had to earn. If homework wasn't completed and returned, recess wasn't earned. The problem was that there were students who didn't want to go to recess in the first place.

9

STUDENT ATTENDANCE

"I still remember when you and I would always talk in the morning."

If a school wants to improve in areas such as graduation rates, test scores, and their overall academic program, one of the first places to look is student attendance. Many schools have policies in place determining required days in class, and follow up with students and their families if absences become a concern. How about students who are in school, but late on a consistent basis? For some families, kids, even at a young age, are responsible for getting themselves up, dressed, fed, and on their way to school. Is this fair? Most of us would say no, but that's the way it is.

Classroom Tales...

I remember one third grade student telling me that she was absent from school the day before because Mom took her shopping.

. . .

One year, one of my fifth grade girls was absent on the first Friday and the following Tuesday. The other students and the office confirmed that this was typical. It seems that Mom left for work before the bus came and it was up to her to get herself ready for school. I decided to establish a very supportive, positive school environment for her so she would want to come to school each day. I even tried to be "charming" as I built a relationship with her.

In our parent/student handbook, it was clearly stated that students were expected to be in school each day except for sickness, etc. and vacations should be scheduled when school was out. One night, after a school board meeting, a board member came up to apologize to me because his child was going to be in Florida for a week when school was in session.

I have to be honest when it comes to student attendance. I took it personally when students in my class were absent from school. I know that sounds silly, but it's true.

There's a student we have now and you just know his parents tell him what to say when we ask why he wasn't in school. It's frustrating because it's clear that the parents let him know that school isn't a priority.

I had a boy in fifth grade who came from a very difficult home situation where few rules existed and he and his siblings were "on their own" quite a bit. He'd occasionally come to school exhausted and fall asleep in class.

...and Lessons Learned

I have to admit that if a particularly difficult child was absent, there was a part of me that felt a sigh of relief. That being said, as the professional, a teacher has to do everything in their power to project the image that every student should be in school every day and on time because attending school is important. If you, as the teacher don't believe that, then neither will your students or their parents.

Make sure that any missed work is made up and communicate those expectations to the child's parents. If a child is absent, try to arrange for the work to be sent home with a sibling, a friend, or a neighbor. If possible, inquire as to whether a parent can pick up the homework. In other words, make it clear that school attendance is important to the child's success.

Depending on the student and situation, it may be more effective to emphasize the importance of good attendance by sympathizing with the student. Ask why he/she was absent, not in an accusing voice but one of concern. Let them know you missed them and offer to help them catch up on the important work they missed because, of course, that important work must be done.

Even with good intentions, you can't really expect students to maintain a good attendance record if your attendance as a teacher is "spotty". Like in many aspects of school, you have to model the behavior that you expect from students.

Classroom teachers, the school nurse, and even the principal should recognize good attendance through awards, etc. and follow up poor attendance with phone calls home and letters written. It may be true that phone calls and letters can be ignored, but it's not as easy to ignore a registered letter that requires a signature, and, yes, I used this strategy more than once as a principal.

10

BATHROOM

"Hopefully, I will see you in stores."

A pet peeve of mine was when we were in the middle of a lesson and I asked a question pertaining to the topic. A student would raise their hand with the intent, I thought, to answer the question or contribute to the discussion in some way. Instead it was "Can I go to the bathroom?". That drove me crazy.

When it comes to students and teachers using a school bathroom it seems simple enough. Someone has to use the restroom so they get up and go. Oh, if it were only that simple.

I suppose that problems with students using the bathroom begin with when they can go. If kids can leave the classroom whenever they feel like it, there'll be a crowd in the restroom in no time, with kids from different classes arranging to get together at a set time (no, I'm not kidding). Some students will also head to the bathroom numerous times throughout the day, whether for "legitimate reasons", or to take a break from a certain subject, to avoid a test, etc.

Because of situations like these, teachers come up with brilliant strategies to limit bathroom visits for their students. Sign out sheets, bathroom tags, scheduled visits, and limiting the number of visits per day are all tried and true strategies, but none work all of the time. Bathroom "problems", by the way, include many that haven't changed in decades. Kids still climb on the stall walls, empty the soap dispenser all over, clog the toilet, break ceiling tiles, and bully other students.

Teachers using school bathrooms shouldn't really be a problem, but there are two concerns worth mentioning. First, what does a teacher do if they need to use the restroom and there is no one to supervise their class? Do you just leave your class for a few minutes? The second problem is when adults use student restrooms. It may not be a concern, but then again...

Classroom Tales...

A teacher I knew wouldn't allow certain students to use the bathroom when they asked because she was sure they didn't need to go and were just trying to get out of class. More than one kid had an accident in that classroom.

One of my third grade girls left art class with permission to go to the restroom down the hall. She was a "high spirited" student and when she got there, someone was already in a stall so she decided to see who it was by sliding under the door. It was a teacher and not a teacher who saw any humor in this at all.

One of my third graders, before he could get to the bathroom, decided to "projectile vomit", hitting my desk, the floor, the garbage can (his intended "target"), etc. I handled it well- which means I didn't throw up myself.

. . .

Decades of teaching have convinced me that flushing a toilet should be part of the school curriculum. Enough said.

I had to go into the boys room (I'm a female) when I heard this blood curdling scream. The water had come out all over the floor and a student had slipped and banged his leg. Here I am, trying to comfort him while realizing that I'm a woman in a boy's bathroom.

I tried to have "common sense" bathroom rules in my classroom using tags but also making it clear that students should try to avoid going to the bathroom when I was teaching a lesson- unless it was an emergency. One year a student in my third grade class had an accident the first or second day of class because he wasn't sure what constituted an emergency.

When I was an assistant principal, the principal told me the bathroom in the hall was for administrators only and was to be used only by the two of us. As it turned out, there was no other bathroom for teachers on that side of the building so I left the door unlocked for others to use. I was reminded in no uncertain terms that this restroom was only for "us" and was to remain locked.

After an overflowing toilet flooded part of our school overnight the secretary announced over the public address system that I had drowned- she was joking, of course, but quite a few students became very upset and she had to quickly go back on the PA system to share that it was just a joke.

. . .

We used charter buses for really long trips and these had bathrooms on board, but as a rule, I never used the bathroom on the bus. There were too many things that students could do when I was in there.

...and Lessons Learned

On the very first day of school- not the second or third- make sure each of your students knows where the bathroom is and what your procedures are for them to use it. That may seem obvious, or even silly, but most classes are either in a different location in your school than the kids are used to or you may have children new to the school. By the way, even though you may have a great deal of information to share on that first day, your students are more interested in "practical" info, such as what the bathroom rules are.

It may seem as if parents are not involved in students using the school bathroom, but having a good relationship with them can help in this area. Students may have medical reasons as to why they need more restroom visits or parents may be able to help if their child seems to be using it "too often" without a legitimate reason.

Regardless of your "bathroom procedures", make your expectations clear as to what's expected from your students. I'd always let my kids know that if I couldn't trust them to use the bathroom appropriately by third grade, we had real problems. In other words, let your students know that they are "above" bad bathroom behavior.

I liked to use two bathroom tags, one for boys and one for girls. If a student needed to use the restroom, the student simply took the tag and placed it on their desk. This method worked because, at a glance, I knew which students were out of the room, it limited this to two students, and

I didn't have to be interrupted. On the other hand, one or more students sometimes needed to go to the bathroom at the same time and would be staring at the tag on a desk, getting ready to race to grab it first instead of doing their work. Of course, there were also emergencies.

I always told my students that if going to the bathroom was an emergency to just get up and go. They didn't need to get the tag or ask me. This worked pretty well because I was usually teaching small groups or the entire class and the student didn't have to interrupt me or wait. I did encourage them to tell a friend where they were going so I would be told at the first opportunity. This also worked with a student who felt as if they were about to be sick.

11

STUDENT RESPONSIBILITIES

Students often forgot to write their last name on papers. I'd ask them if they went to the "Beyonce and Prince School of First Names Only".

"The project that I liked was the castle project because I like painting and there was a lot of painting involved."

Schools revolve around instruction and learning, and the responsibilities given to students and the resulting expectations go a long way towards determining how successful each student will be. This is an especially difficult process for many younger elementary children because these kids are just beginning to become "academic learners", and accepting the responsibilities that go along with being a student is a big challenge. In the meantime, teachers know that every child is different, yet we have to maintain certain standards for all of our students.

Classroom Tales...

I had a fifth grade student who never wasted a second. If I let the class know that we'd be going to lunch in three minutes, she would get a book out for three minutes. If she was done with a class assignment, she got out something else to do without needing to be told or given the suggestion. I still wish I was more like her.

One little girl said she didn't have her homework because Mom didn't pack it for her and I asked whose fault that was. She admitted, with a bit of an attitude, that it was her fault. A few minutes later, I heard her call me an "old woman".

We had a castle building project and one boy clearly completed this project the night before, even though he had a month to do it. It showed.

I had three boys who really struggled with organizing their things. Luckily, I had three girls who were excellent students and helped the boys fill out their homework agenda and keep their materials organized. I should've paid them.

I used a job chart and I had a lot of jobs for kids, one of which was to write the homework on the board. Well, I color coordinated all of my copies by subject and a student who didn't spell very well went up to the board and wrote under science "Green Sh*t". I noticed it and walked across the room as casually as possible to erase it. I'm not sure how many students wrote it down that way, but no parents contacted me.

.   .   .

"My homework is done, but I left it at home" was always followed by me saying, "Then it's not done."

One boy had a cubby that was absolutely disgusting, even though we checked all of the cubbies once a week. At Easter, we did an Easter egg hunt and I hid an egg in that boy's cubby.

Some of us noticed an odor in our class that seemed to get worse over a number of days. When it became almost unbearable, I decided to call our custodian when a thought occurred to me. I asked my students if any of them had forgotten to bring home the bathing suit they had used when we had been swimming several weeks earlier. One of the girls sheepishly raised her hand.

...and Lessons Learned

Make sure any consequence you give for students being irresponsible is less preferable than being responsible in the first place.

As an elementary teacher, it was important that I taught and modeled responsible behavior in terms of work habits, relationships with others, etc. That being said, none of us are perfect and we sometimes fall far short in modeling responsible behavior for children.

Completing long term projects is a very difficult skill for children and many adults. Give kids every chance to succeed, with regular reminders, both written and verbal, and make sure parents are also well aware of what their children are responsible for.

. . .

Parents need to find a balance between helping their children and doing their work for them. Make the parental role clear in the beginning of the year, communicate often with parents, and, most difficult, be ready to address parents if they step over the line in "helping" their child.

12

THE SCHOOL CAFETERIA

In the cafeteria, one student frantically raised their hand and shouted "Mrs. S., we have pictures today! We've got to get these kids cleaned up and outta here!"

The school cafeteria was about much more than food. After recess and gym class, this was the place in school that most students looked forward to visiting more than any other. Kids often had more of a choice regarding seating and what foods they ate and- most important in my opinion- they had a period of time when they didn't have to listen to the same adult tell them what they had to do every minute.

Classroom Tales...

I was sitting in my office as a new principal enjoying, with a fair degree of nervousness, the first day of school when one of the loudest noises I've ever heard sounded. It was from a "traffic light" mounted on the wall in our cafeteria and it went off when the kids were too loud. Quite honestly, it scared the hell out of me!

One year our district instituted a policy requiring kids who owed money in the cafeteria to be given a peanut butter and jelly sandwich for lunch each day until their bill was paid off. We were angry about this because the kids who owed money were singled out and because it was up to their parents to pay- after all, we were talking about elementary students here. Some of us would approach the cashier at quiet times, find out who owed money, and pay off their bill. One of our teaching assistants gave $100 towards what students owed.

While on cafeteria duty, a student called me over because a classmate was choking on a mozzarella stick. The student couldn't speak and couldn't dislodge it so I did the Heimlich and thank God it worked! Scary as all get out! We were both shaking and near tears after that.

I worked in a school where students were not allowed to get out of their seats for any reason once they sat down. If they forgot a spoon, a napkin, or whatever, it didn't matter. It wasn't that they had to ask permission- it's that they weren't allowed to get what they had forgotten in the first place, and if a student did approach the counter to get something, screaming occurred.

I was subbing and the class was getting their things to go to the cafeteria. One boy burst into tears while claiming that another boy "stole" his snack. Later, after lunch, the two boys approached me to say that they had resolved the problem with the one boy admitting that he did, indeed, take the other boy's snack and he bought a second bag of the snack to make up for it.

.   .   .

One student refused to eat because he only liked peanut butter and jelly on white bread, but the cafeteria had to include one piece of white and one piece of wheat bread with each sandwich because of some nutritional guidelines.

One of my boys was sitting at his table in the cafeteria when another boy brought his hand up to the students face quickly to scare him and he fell off his seat. The young man who fell was a very nervous boy who would "shut down" at times when uncomfortable, and since he wouldn't tell the lunchroom monitor what had happened, he was sent to the principal, not as a punishment, but because he wouldn't speak to the monitor. Well, he wouldn't speak to the principal either.

My niece and nephew went to an elementary school that had a "silent lunch time". No talking was allowed at all.

One year, I supervised the cafeteria in my elementary school. We developed a "rewards program" and I would meet with the lunchroom monitors once a week to go over any problems or questions. Kids who had been written up for bad behavior would be sent to my fifth grade classroom at a certain time when I would go over the unacceptable behavior and give any consequences, such as sitting in my room during their recess. I was teaching math at this time and my class was always interested in how I could change my demeanor to a different level for this task.

...and Lessons Learned

Teachers in some schools are assigned to cafeteria duty, where they monitor student behavior, eating habits, etc. There are advantages to this, including seeing students in a more relaxed environment than the classroom (I actually enjoyed this time with my kids and encouraged better eating habits and expectations regarding manners) and using your authority as teachers to ensure a more orderly location. The problem with this is that it harms the image of teachers as professionals and takes them away from instructional tasks that they are better suited for. In short, tax payer dollars are not being used effectively.

During the majority of my teaching years, lunchtime for students was 30 minutes long and recess was scheduled at a different time and length by the teacher. I sub in schools where lunch and recess is a 20 + 20 minute combination, which I like because most kids don't need 30 minutes to eat and most problems occurred in the later part of lunch time when kids were finished eating and had nothing to do.

I'm going to sound "old school" here, but I expect kids to take care of their own garbage, trays, etc. I was told recently that it's just easier for an adult to do it, but to me, it just seems like another example of eliminating responsibility and lowering expectations.

There certainly needs to be rules and procedures in a school cafeteria, but this is also a time for kids to enjoy a needed break from the classroom. Whoever supervises the lunchroom has to strike a balance so kids get to unwind a little while still following school rules.

13

THE SCHOOL SECRETARY

"You and I had lots of great times together."

If you really want to know what goes on in school, don't ask a teacher or a student or even the principal. Ask the school secretary. Part of this is certainly the physical location of where the secretary is stationed, which is usually in a space that is central to where visitors enter the school and near the office of the building administrator. However, there is more to it.

Just about everything that happens in a school goes though the secretary in the office. This includes greeting visitors, handling all communications, and being privy to confidential information. Depending on the role the building administrator plays in a school, which really does vary quite a bit depending on the district and the working style of the principal, the secretary may be the "point person" on many issues. Secretaries sometimes handle student discipline, assign substitute teachers, decide whether recess is inside or outside, and even check report cards before they are sent home with students. In other words, secretaries are really the "jack of all trades" in a school.

Classroom Tales...

I had a conversation with a principal once who gave me some advice. He said to never work as a building administrator in a school where the secretary was "mean and nasty"- those words are a cleaner version of what he said.

A secretary I know was sent by the principal to tell a classroom teacher that she couldn't show a certain movie to her students because it wasn't appropriate. It wasn't something the principal wanted to do, so...

I had this habit of losing my attendance envelope, usually leaving it in a colleague's room when visiting. Our school secretary would often call out to me about it as I walked past the office with my students. Once, when it was missing for several days, I tried to crouch down among the kids, hoping she wouldn't see me, when I heard that loud voice suggesting I was in trouble again. But it turns out that she had my envelope the whole time.

It's rarely easy working side by side with others in an office and this was especially true when two secretaries in my school were related.

A teacher sent a student down to the office in tears because he had supposedly stolen some toys from classmates. He assured the secretary that he didn't steal anything and she placed the toys on her desk while he sat nearby. After answering a phone call she turned around and the toys were gone.

. . .

A little girl in second grade had not heard from her mother in eighteen months when the Mom called the office and asked to speak to her daughter because she was going into surgery and wanted her daughter to know. Mom cried and was so scared....we had to give her a boost (not permitting her to talk to her daughter) and told her when she was better to come in and see us. She called back three times. It's hard being the secretary at times.

One secretary I knew who was the main school secretary, but worked with two other secretaries, referred to them as "her girls". They hated it.

...and Lessons Learned

Secretaries know everything that goes on in a school and, if they've been there even a short while, they also know every family, relationship, and individual who lives in the school community. This may seem intrusive to some, but there are countless times when this knowledge comes in handy if you're a teacher or principal.

If you're a teacher, don't get on the bad side of the school secretary. If you're the principal, don't get on the bad side of the school secretary. By the way, this lesson also applies to the school custodian.

I suppose this is up to school administrators, but the tasks assigned to a school secretary need to be clearly defined. Too many times, this individual is treated as a "substitute principal".

. . .

There's a day in the calendar that used to be called "Secretaries Day" and I believe it's now called "Administrative Assistants Day". Regardless of what it's called, don't forget to recognize this day with a card, flowers, lunch, a gift certificate, etc.

14

MEET THE TEACHER NIGHT

"I really miss you and your extremely long and boring stories."

"The funny thing about you is when you told GREAT funny stories about your family and friends."

Most schools I'm familiar with schedule an event in the fall designed to bring parents and teachers together so information can be shared and effective communication established. Whether it's called Meet the Teacher Night, Open House, Curriculum Night, etc. doesn't really matter because the goals remain the same. Parents get to meet their child's teachers, kids take their parents on a school "tour", and teachers share information on how their classroom operates.

The two biggest issues faced are planning the format for the evening and getting as many parents as possible to attend. The format is easy in one way- there is no perfect format. Should students be included or just parents? Will the event be held on one evening or will different grade levels hold theirs on different nights? Will there be formal presentations by teachers or will parents just "wander around"?

Getting parents to attend is made easier if you balance convenience, value, and guilt. Yes, GUILT. Give parents plenty of notice so they can adjust schedules and make sure that the event provides information crucial to their child's success in school. Let parents know repeatedly that they are EXPECTED to attend, and if they truly care about their child's education, they'll be there.

Classroom Tales...

One year, we held a "Curriculum Night" just for parents- there were more teachers there than parents, and we were pretty depressed.

Because I tend to "ramble on", I would give the "gong" to one of my students when I started speaking. When my designated time was up, no more than 15 minutes, the student would hit the gong and I would stop speaking immediately. Parents knew they wouldn't have to sit there listening to me go on and the kids were motivated to be there to see who would get the gong and watch me when it sounded.

We tried making the gym available as "child care" so parents could focus on the teacher presenting in their kid's classroom. Ask the gym teachers how their night went after two to three hundred kids ran around the gym for an hour and a half.

When our special area teachers had to speak in the auditorium and in front of 200 parents as they gave a brief description of their program, our art teacher, as she walked up to the microphone, leaned down and whispered to me that she was going to have a heart attack at any moment- she didn't, and was fantastic!

· · ·

I usually served cookies and juice after I was done speaking. Food ALWAYS works- except that you have spills, the cookies are gone in 2 minutes, and kids that aren't even in your class come in for a snack!

When I was a principal, a mom called to say that she wanted to be there, but couldn't find any way to leave her child at home. She wanted to know if I would be mad if she brought her child since it was the only way she could attend.

I enjoyed Meet The Teacher Night, but I didn't enjoy speaking in front of parents. I get tongue tied and very nervous. After a few years of this I told parents that I wasn't going to do a formal speech, but I would answer questions and speak to parents one on one. I put all the books and everything out and did things that way from then on.

I had my students introduce me to their parents at "Meet the Teacher" night. We practiced a day or two before so they knew to say "Mr. Sack, this is my Mom, Frances, and my Dad, Ray. Mom and Dad, this is Mr. Sack." Most were pretty good at it, although some would stumble a bit.

...and Lessons Learned

Teachers are trained to work with kids and generally become comfortable speaking in front of a class early in their careers. This is often not so with parents and other adults. Regardless, it is imperative that "Meet the Teacher Night" be more than parents just wandering around a classroom looking at their child's work and where their desk is. Just as the first day of school is when a teacher sets the tone with a new class, this evening is when the teacher sets the tone for parents, making expectations clear, sharing rules and procedures, showing materials to be used in instruction, etc.

.   .   .

Parents would sometimes approach me and share private information as if this was a parent/teacher conference, even though other
parents and children were close by. Many would also ask how their
child was doing and this made kids incredibly nervous. I had already
assured my students that I wouldn't share any negative info at this
type of event, so my stock answer to parents was that their child was
doing fine, was adjusting well to many new things, etc.

When I attended Meet the Teacher Night as a parent, the classroom
teacher explained that the Math textbook wasn't very good, but the
district was too cheap to buy a better series. Another time, as a
special education teacher I rotated with my students and their
parents to different classes to hear from the subject areas when the
social studies teacher stated that she knew social studies was pretty
boring, but she would do her best. These are not comments or opinions that should be shared with parents or students.

Speaking of presentations, there is often a struggle in schools as to
the importance of special areas of instruction, such as art, physical
education, music, etc. In my experience, teachers in these areas can
feel less appreciated or less important than classroom teachers. This
is a primary reason why these teachers must also be required to do a
short presentation for parents. This may be hard to fit into a schedule, but it is very important that these programs be viewed as an inte-
gral part of a child's curriculum and this starts with sharing a
summary of the curriculum and expectations with parents.

15

DISMISSAL

"I love the fact that I was in your last class."

If ever there would be an easy process in a school, you'd think it would be dismissal. Bring your students to the classroom door or directly to their bus and wave goodbye. What could be simpler than that?

My guess is that dismissal time when I was in elementary school back in the 60's was more complicated than it appeared. Now, though, there are multiple factors to consider including who is picking up the child, changes in the normal bus routine, how weather affects buses, walkers, and parents picking up their children when after school programs and extra curricular activities occur. Still, the goal at dismissal time remains the same, and that is to ensure that every student reaches their planned destination safely.

Classroom Tales...

In a district I was working in, buses parked all over the parking lot
and not just in a row for buses only. School personnel would guide a
line of children as they weaved between, behind, and in front of
buses until they reached the appropriate bus. Cars were also in the
parking lot at this time, although they weren't supposed to be
moving. One day, one of our teaching assistants threw herself on the
hood of a moving car as students walked to their buses.

I worked in a school that required each classroom teacher to lead
their children out to the buses at dismissal time. This seemed to be a
fair and effective procedure. Some teachers began complaining,
though, when it turned out that two of their colleagues who worked
together were taking turns, with that day's teacher walking out two
classes instead of just their own. The two teachers in question had
made a separate arrangement with the principal.

One parent, who had a history of being argumentative, would send
her older child who attended high school to pick up his younger
sibling even though school policy stated that no child could be
released in the custody of a minor. The mom didn't care and was
always ready for a fight over this.

At the end of almost every school day we would hear an announcement listing bus substitutions, such as Bus 94 is Bus 76 today. There
was a long list each day and students would always ask me which bus
they had to take. Luckily, I had fifth graders and I'd always tell them
that I drove to school, so they better pay attention. Looking back, that
was kind of mean.

·   ·   ·

As a principal, I had two kids stay with me after school for an hour when there was a mixup in which parent was picking them up. Luckily, we had snacks. I even shared, which I thought was pretty generous of me.

I taught until the end of the day and then my students filled in their agenda with that night's homework assignments before packing up. I didn't appreciate a phone call at the end of the day to tell me that "Ralph" was getting picked up and I needed to send him down "now". Ralph didn't get there "now".

When I was subbing, three girls had an issue with going to the house of one of the girls. There were notes from home about this, but one of the kids didn't want another of the girls to go. Calls were made from school to all three families to get it sorted out. When we thought it was taken care of and one of the girls was told to just take her regular bus, the issue then became that she didn't usually take the bus on Fridays.

There was a birthday party planned one day and a parent sent in a list of approximately 12 kids that should take her child's (he was the birthday boy) bus to their house.

...and Lessons Learned

Schools need to establish rules regarding dismissal and stick to them. Get ready for arguments and phone calls, though, some of which will be directed to the Superintendent or Board of Education members.

Encourage parents to stick to a schedule regarding dismissal. Kids often go to different parents, guardians, or other destinations after school depending on the day, the week, etc. These changes are tough on kids and school personnel.

An early dismissal for any reason is exciting, but also a nightmare for everyone. Be prepared just in case.

An easy way to score "brownie points" if you are an administrator is to dismiss teachers as soon as students are gone on bad weather days. Teachers are nervous on these days as well, worried about driving on slippery roads, their own children getting to where they need to be, etc. Keeping teachers in school on these days based on their contractual day is viewed as insensitive and those affected often feel as if they are not valued.

16

PARENT RESPONSIBILITIES

A common pet peeve among teachers is when parents make excuses for their children.

"In third grade you have been a cool rocking teacher even though I've been in trouble."

Most teachers and parents recognize the need for a partnership to exist in order for a child to be successful in school. The role of parents in this partnership seems to have changed over the years, even though teacher's expectations for parents probably haven't. Consistent attendance, appropriate dress, homework completed and checked, and lunch or money to purchase a school lunch- these are the responsibilities of parents as part of this home/school partnership. At least that's the way it's supposed to work.

Classroom Tales...

I can't tell you how many times kids came to school in the winter without hats, gloves, and jackets. Our nurse always had a stockpile of extra clothes and kids always wanted to head down to her office to borrow things so they could go out for recess. One of my third grade girls asked to do this, but by the time she went to the nurse, found things to wear, and headed outside, recess was over.

I had a third grade boy who was late almost every day. It was his job to get himself ready and to wake Mom, but he wasn't always motivated to do that.

One morning, one of my students, a sweet little blond hair, freckled face boy, took a deep breath and said, "Boy, it was a rough night last night. My family went to see Uncle Joe... well, he's not really my uncle but for some reason we call him uncle. Well, my father kept drinking "liquids" and more "liquids" and FINALLY Mom said he'd had enough and we'd better leave. So Dad said he would drive home and Mom said no, but he still said he would. Along the way home we saw flashing lights and a cop pulled us over. Well, (deep breath), when the cop made dad get out of the car a beer can fell out. So after making Dad walk around funny for awhile, the cop gave him a ticket and said Mom had to drive home. Mom was REALLY mad and said, "And when we get home, I am going to flush those "tomato" plants down the toilet, too. I don't know why she would flush good plants, but I was so tired I just went to bed when we got home. So if I misbehave today, it is probably because I am tired."

One of our third grade projects was building a castle while we were studying Europe. Each student would show their castle to the class and explain how they built it, what materials they used, etc. One student stood up and announced that she didn't know anything about her castle because her Dad had told her to go out and play while he built her castle.

One year, we had a new kindergarten student move into the district in January. On his first day, Dad pulled up to the curb, let the boy climb out of the car and close the door, and then drove off. Pretty tough start for a five year old walking into a new school and not knowing anyone.

...and Lessons Learned

The goal in school is for a working relationship to exist between school and home. Part of this is for parents to understand their responsibilities and, when it comes to education, it is the responsibility of educators to make parental responsibilities clear.

Being a good role model isn't always easy, but when you became a parent it's a job that you accepted. Concerning your child's education, that means getting your child to school ready to learn and supporting his/her efforts.

In our student agendas, which went back and forth every day with every student, there was a parent handbook section. It included separate lists of 5-6 specific responsibilities for teachers, students and parents. Since parents were expected to sign this section, it was made clear that parents had responsibilities in their child's education.

I always found it very frustrating dealing with parents who openly criticized their former spouses, especially in front of their children. I tried to understand the emotions, but my job was to be the best teacher I could be for their kids. Teachers have to decide whether to ignore the negative comments parents make regarding the other person or to speak up and let parents know how those comments can affect children.

I understand how difficult it is for parents to look at every test paper, notice from school, etc., especially when you have more than one child. I also know that you'd need a refrigerator that was twelve feet wide to display everything. Still, parents need to go through their child's backpack on a regular basis because it will help them to see how their child is doing academically and be aware of what's happening in school.

17

HALLOWEEN

"You really don't sing very well, Mrs. S."
"Yes, I know, but I enjoy singing songs with you all."
"No. You REALLY don't sing well!"

The beginning of October is the time of year to get ready for Halloween in school. Elementary students are thinking about their costumes, and teachers begin making plans for a classroom party and thinking about whether they also would be dressing up. Administrators are dealing with upcoming school wide parades and hordes of parents attending that day to see their kids in the parade and to be at the classroom party later on. At least, that's the way I remember most of my Halloweens in school.

Classroom Tales...

I usually dressed up for Halloween because the kids liked it, even though it's not something I'm totally comfortable doing. I tried to use costumes that were "homemade" so kids saw that it was not all about money. The best? I went as a laundry basket once by cutting out the bottom of a basket so I could stand inside and then clothes were piled in and socks and shirts and things were "velcroed" to me. The worst? I tried to go as a bag of leaves by taking a big leaf bag and cutting holes for my legs before filling it with leaves. As I walked, the bag started ripping and leaves began dropping in the hallway- you should have seen the custodian's face!

I love Halloween! Usually, the team dressed as a theme. One year we dressed in blow up costumes. There was Elvis, a ballerina, a sumo wrestler, and others. The kids loved it!

When I was a principal, we held a Halloween dance for our 6th graders, most of whom wore costumes. One girl came as a murder victim. The student had a fake scar with blood on her neck and makeup to make her look as if she was dead.

I loved Halloween when I was first teaching. The staff worked as teams to brainstorm their themed costumes and the kids were so proud of their own costumes as they paraded past parents, staff, and other students. I was fortunate to work with a principal who made sure we had costumes available for those students who were unable to provide their own, and he also had some spectacularly creative ones. Our school developed such a sense of community on those "whole school celebration days"!

My favorite Halloween tie had a vampire saying "I **vant** to drink your blood". No matter how many kids read that tie, almost all of them read it as "I **want** to drink your blood". I had to explain it with an excellent vampire voice, if I do say so myself.

·   ·   ·

We did "dunking for apples" in my class each year and also hung donuts from the ceiling. Each student had to put their hands behind their back and eat the donuts from the string.

When I was teaching 5th grade in a K-5 school, there was a parade that travelled throughout the school with parents lined up in the hallways so they could see their kids go by and snap pictures. As the parade got to the end of our school, it then made its way to the elementary school next door- it may have continued on to the middle school because all three schools were connected by hallways. Because we had the "older" kids, the fifth grade teachers just had them join the parade at the end of the line and told them we would see them later when they got back. That was back in the 80s, mind you, and I don't think we worried as much about safety issues then.

Some parents always spent too much on snacks for the class parties. One parent brought in a tray of vegetables and another brought in a tray of fruit. They were beautiful and I appreciated it, but we started asking for smaller contributions, like one kid bringing in a bag of baby carrots, etc.

As we approached Halloween during my first year as principal, I met with a few parents whose image of Halloween was closer to "devil worship" than a day for children to dress up and eat candy.

Because I had a student who didn't celebrate Halloween, I sent home a letter letting parents know that we would be having a "fall festival" instead. One parent who worked in the school walked into my classroom when I was doing a lesson, plopped a snack down on the table, and said "Here!". Evidently, she was angry and had an attitude like "How dare you not have snacks or food for Halloween?".

...and Lessons Learned

I'm torn between what I consider the "school tradition" of allowing kids to dress up for Halloween and parading through the school vs. recognizing time constraints, safety concerns with so many visitors, issues with snacks, and the general disruption of the school day. In the end, I believe that school is more than work and testing. School can provide a safe, fun environment for kids to enjoy this holiday and, especially considering the current culture, using part of the school day is a good trade off.

Regardless of whether a school celebrates Halloween, don't allow parents or other visitors to dress up in costumes. Younger kids, especially, can be scared of strangers in costumes, especially scary looking ones, and it's much harder to be aware of who's visiting your school when individuals show up with masks on.

Most years I'd have a student whose parent wanted to come in to my classroom to help their child with makeup or to get into their costume. I didn't allow this because it added just one more distraction to an already "busy" day.

It sounds easy, but I had one simple rule in my class on days such as Halloween. That rule, which students heard several times leading up to the day we had our party and parade, was that we would have plenty of fun during those special events, but the rest of the day was business as usual. I didn't want to hear about the party or see kids playing with costume pieces until the appropriate time. This policy worked well for holidays and for other special days, also.

. . .

When it came to buses, which most of my students took each day, I felt it was a distraction to have students wear their costumes on the bus. I explained to them that I wanted the driver to concentrate on the road and not on students in costumes acting silly. This was sometimes difficult for kids in more complicated costumes, but safety was more important and I believe most children and parents understood that.

On days such as Halloween, dismissal can be very difficult. There's the volume of adults, custody arrangements to verify, etc. That brings me to the following:

There are many ways to organize Halloween activities in school, including parades, parties, costumes, snacks, and transportation. The single most important lesson I've learned is that school personnel must communicate clearly regarding expectations. Parents and children need to know what's expected of them and they need to know early. If these expectations are shared in notices sent home, on the school website, etc. the day will go much smoother.

18

MY FAVORITE TEACHER

Student: "Miss B. I have a secret." Miss. B. "What's your secret?" Student: "I like you."

I was an Adjunct Professor at an area college teaching classes on education. On the first or second night of class, I asked each student to write down the names of their former teachers, beginning with kindergarten, and most had no trouble doing so. I'm 65 now, and I don't have a good memory, but I have no trouble remembering the names of my teachers, especially those from elementary school.

I share this because I truly believe that teachers have a tremendous influence on children that lasts much longer than the year that student and teacher spent together. We tend to remember the book read aloud, the special projects, funny jokes, or the way math was taught. Many of us became educators because of that "favorite teacher".

Classroom Tales...

In high school, we somehow got onto the topic of death. Being the youngest in the family, and not the prettiest or most popular in school, I figured I would die alone. I'd never marry and my parents and siblings would go before me. I went to my French teacher and asked, "When I die, will you come to my funeral?" He never hesitated, laughed, or tried to reason with me. He looked me straight in the eye and said, "Of course, I'll come." His kindness still makes my heart smile.

When third grade ended, the name on my report card for fourth grade was Mrs. S., who was my brother's teacher and we all heard how great she was. When I got to the classroom on the first day of school, there stood a man teacher. My heart sank. None of us knew what to think. From that first day, I knew he was going to be a great teacher by the way he talked and asked us to think. He turned out to be my favorite teacher. He was kind, smart, thought provoking, creative, helpful and he was my first man teacher.

I suppose quite a few students get crushes on their teacher at one time or another. For me, it was Miss C., my French teacher in high school. I wasn't a very good student, and that included French class. However, since Miss C. offered extra help, I made it a point to attend those "help" sessions and never missed French class. I was heart-broken when she got married in the spring. At the end of the year, she wrote a lengthy message in my yearbook in French and, to this day, I have no idea what it says. I like to think it was a request to run off together, but it probably wasn't.

My music teacher was a favorite because he cared about students and didn't seem as if he was coming to school for the paycheck. He was tough and expected a lot out of us, but he was also someone we could talk to.

It was my first day of school and my first gym class. Mr. L. was the teacher and it was love at first sight! Everything we did was everything I was good at. I remember all the skills and games we worked on, and went home to tell my Mom that I wanted to be a gym teacher. I was five and never in all my years did I ever change my mind. I had the chance to tell Mr. L. this many years later at a track meet. He was so happy to see me...and he remembered my name! I still love teaching after thirty-eight years and I'm still happy with the choice I made when I was five!

My favorite teacher was my fourth grade teacher. She had a love of reading, writing, and science like me and was also very kind, which is a good thing to see in a teacher.

My favorite teacher was my senior year social studies teacher. Ms. G's teaching style and personality had a large impact on me- a shy, insecure student. I was full of anxiety, far too self-conscious and very hard on myself. Ms. G made me feel important, not invisible as I felt in many other classes, and I became a more capable student. Ms. G wasn't judgmental and expected her students to be respectful towards her because she had <u>earned</u> it. In return, she respected her students. Years later I was able to dine with Ms. G. and express just how important her influence was on me. I sit here now at my computer with a framed political button collection on my wall. That collection was given to me by Ms. G. and I treasure it.

My favorite teacher was in 4th grade and I gave her a hug every day before I went home. I don't know why she was my favorite- there was just something about the way she taught us and she just took me under her wing. To this day, I think that's why 4th grade is my favorite.

...and Lessons Learned

Most teachers probably know this, but being a favorite teacher can't be your goal. You do your job to the best of your ability and try to be the best teacher you can be. Most kids will respond to your effort and some may always remember you as their favorite!

Elementary teachers have an advantage here as most students automatically like their teacher. I worked with many teachers over the years and, although the majority did their best and sincerely enjoyed teaching, there were a few that were just unpleasant toward their students and unhappy when teaching. In my experience, their students liked them anyway.

The characteristics that "favorite teachers" seem to have in common are mostly personal. They suggest someone who is compassionate and who cares about his/her students as individuals. It isn't just about effective teaching, it's about the personal bond that forms between teacher and student.

19

TEACHER RESPONSIBILITIES

"I can't tell you how much you helped me to become who I am today. I have a 92.667 average. Even though I can't spell, I figure things out."

"What is the role of a teacher?" This was often asked at teacher workshops, I think, as a way of opening up the discussion. We would then begin listing things such as parent, counselor, doctor/nurse, coach, mediator, etc. That was in earlier decades. Now?

I've always viewed teachers as the individuals who shape not only our children now, but future leaders, professionals, parents, etc. As a teacher I took a back seat to no one when I viewed what I did for a living. That hasn't changed. Good teachers deserve every ounce of respect because they earn it.

That being said, teachers have responsibilities just like students and parents when it comes to school and education. I don't think anyone thinks it's enough for a teacher to go through the motions with students. As there has been an increased level of scrutiny and criticism of teachers shared publicly, it is more difficult and even more important that teachers continue to fulfill their professional responsibilities.

Classroom Tales...

The teacher next door had a classroom that impressed anyone who saw it. I myself was quite insulted when teachers walked around before open house, visited her room, and then asked me what had happened to my room.

As a principal, I made an announcement over the public address system on most Fridays letting teachers know that the school would be open Saturday morning and they were welcome to join me. I was never alone.

A friend took a week off from school when an amazing opportunity came up for her to travel abroad. She asked me if I thought she should just take the days as sick/personal days or approach the administrator and explain the situation honestly, which is what I recommended. The result wasn't what she had hoped for.

I worked for a number of years with a fifth grade teacher who always seemed happy when in front of his students. I never saw him appear as if he didn't want to be there. He always had a great attitude toward teaching!

I worked in a district that was filled with negativity between teachers, administrators, and Board of Education members. It was so bad that there was a newsletter, written anonymously, that was posted in each school in the district about every month or so filled with mean and vulgar comments about district employees. I still have a copy of one.

. . .

One summer when I was a principal we had several new teachers that had been hired. I remember pulling into the parking lot one August day to see one of them painting bookshelves that she had carried outside from her classroom. Another burst into tears when she found out that the building would be closed over the Labor Day weekend and she couldn't get in to work in her classroom.

I worked with a teacher who was as kind and gentle with her students as she was with colleagues. I never heard a negative comment or saw a negative response. One day I noticed her staring at a teacher from a different school in the district with total disgust. She told me how that person had been her teacher in high school and on the first day of school, he had pulled out her chair when she went to sit down, causing her to fall on the floor, absolutely embarrassed. She never forgot that moment.

I considered myself to be a positive role model for my students. That being said, I have to admit that when I became bogged down with papers to correct (my fault), I occasionally would toss a set into the "circular file"- in other words, I threw them out.

Contacting parents is part of the job, whether by note, phone, email, etc. I was a "talker" so I preferred to call, but there were some parents that I really hoped wouldn't answer when I placed that call. I guess that's an advantage with email.

It was a number of years ago when a teacher remarked to me how poor a role model another teacher was because she had a child out of wedlock and she also had a tattoo. This was probably around the year 2010, so we're not talking fifty years ago.

When the nurse called my classroom to say that my daughter had a slight fever and I'd have to take her home, I called the doctor and was told I couldn't even get in for an appointment until 2:30. I told my daughter I'd get my things and leave, but within a few minutes, she had curled up on a bean bag chair and was sound asleep. I let her sleep there and I stayed for the day.

...and Lessons Learned

Like in any profession, teachers must be held accountable for their performance. Most teachers I've known welcomed guidance and evaluation that would help them to improve in their ability as teachers. The key here is that the focus should be on evaluation and improvement, not punishment.

Most students, and even their parents, expect teachers to behave the same whether they are in school or not. That may mean moral standards which many would suggest are unreasonable and teachers may feel that what they do away from school is no one else's business. That being said, teachers have historically been viewed differently because of their role with children. Tread carefully!

It has been my experience that some teachers expect responsible behavior from students while behaving irresponsibly themselves, especially in the way they treat colleagues. None of us are perfect, but we have to serve as positive role models for kids, not only because it's part of our job, but because we may be the only positive role model that many students have.

20

PARENT TEACHER CONFERENCES

One of my pet peeves was the "no show". My students knew that I understood if a parent had to change an appointment, but I became very frustrated if a parent just didn't show up. Parents had my home number, cell number, and the number of the school so I expected a call or note if they couldn't make it.

S ometime in the fall, at least in my experience, schools hold conferences so teachers and their students' parents can discuss the progress being made. Usually, this is a time to examine the first report card and discuss strengths and weaknesses in academics, as well as behavior, attitude, social skills, etc. Ideally, both teacher and parents are comfortable in sharing information and can plan how to move forward with addressing areas in need.

Classroom Tales...

During an evening of parent teacher conferences, the fire alarm went off. Everyone headed outside, where we waited for approximately ten minutes. Just a few minutes after we had resumed conferences inside, the alarm went off again and we again exited the building. After a third time with the alarm going off, we called it a night.

At one conference, a mom came in and, right as we were speaking, her top dentures came out. I tried to pretend like it didn't happen.

When I held evening conferences, I usually stayed in school so I could get some work done before conferences started. I would pick up something for dinner and eat in my room, which worked well except for the lingering odor of subs or Chinese food that parents and kids noticed.

I was teaching in an "open school" and had a few chairs set up as a waiting area. Parents of one student sat down in a different area out of my line of sight and I continued with other parents, assuming that the one family wasn't showing up. About an hour after their scheduled time, they walked over to me, told me they were tired of waiting, and left as I tried to explain.

All I can say about parent/teacher conferences is this- when my mother went to them, she would come home and tell all of us boys that she just gave ALL the teachers permission to "beat us" if we acted up in their class. If the teachers beat you, you will get another one when you got home, also! That is why I was such a good student.

One of the first conferences I attended was as a special education teacher. The parent who attended had very little education and evidently couldn't read because she held the child's report card upside down as she looked it over. It was quite sad.

. . .

As a third grade teacher, I had one student whose older siblings had been my students as well. Getting to school was not an option so we had the conference at their house. I knew the whole family so it was a lot of fun- the kids even made me cookies!

There was one dad who worked at a pizza place and always brought in leftover pizza for us. He thought he was doing something nice, but, since the pizza place was "questionable", we never really ate the pizza.

One of my favorite conferences was with four "parents" of a student. His mom and dad had divorced and each had remarried. All were good friends and all sat down at the conference with me. They stated that their friends thought it was weird that they got along so well and were attending the conference together and asked my opinion. I said that I wished all of my student's parents got along so well.

I was in the middle of a parent teacher conference when I received a phone call from the high school principal's secretary. She stated that I had to speak with the principal right away. Luckily, the parents I was meeting with knew me quite well and assured me it was ok if I returned the call. It turned out that my son had gotten into some trouble with a classmate and the principal felt the need to speak with me immediately.

...and Lessons Learned

Schedule conferences carefully. If you have a parent that goes on forever, don't schedule them last. If there is a student with many issues to discuss, schedule them last.

. . .

The most effective parent/teacher conferences that I ever participated in were when my child sat in and had a part in explaining how he was doing in school. There was a real sense of pride and accountability on the part of my child, and I was able to see first hand the nurturing approach the teacher utilized. Areas of strength and need were discussed in an open manner, with clear expectations for the remainder of the year. As a principal, most parents made a point of expressing their satisfaction to me with their conference when their child was involved.

If you're sticking around school after the regular day until evening conferences begin, it really helps to keep some personal care items handy. A toothbrush and toothpaste, as well as deodorant, should be available. I sometimes also brought another shirt and tie to change into.

The High/Scope method suggests that the first parent teacher meeting be held in a neutral location like a coffee shop- not at school, not at home- so it can be a true partnership. As a parent I found traditional conferences stressful.

Parents need to be made aware of the importance of their attendance and that they are <u>expected</u> to attend. Teachers may not be comfortable projecting this "expectation" so administrators may have to take the lead on this.

Give parents options concerning dates and times, including mornings and evenings. As an educator, you want to offer every opportunity for parents to attend and remove any "excuse" a parent may have for not attending.

. . .

Kids will encourage their parents to attend if they understand from you how important it is <u>and</u> you assure your students that there will be no surprises- they know how they're doing and what their strengths and weaknesses are.

If you have a "Meet the Teacher" night earlier in the year, that is a great time to mention upcoming conferences and to allow parents to sign up for a date and time. They will need a reminder when it gets closer to conference time, but early sign ups allow parents to choose a slot that works best for them and gives you, as a teacher, the right to remind a parent that they've already agreed to attend.

Don't "surround" the parent(s) with 6-8 educators. It can be very intimidating for parents and it's one reason why many do not want to attend or are not comfortable.

Begin the conference with positive comments, whether related to academics, behavior, attitude, etc. You should have no trouble coming up with at least one positive comment to make about a student- ANY student.

Consider the physical set up for conferences. Do you have chairs set up for those who arrive early? Is there student work to see or classroom materials for those waiting to look at?

You should be having a conversation with parents, not talking <u>at</u> them. Do they ask questions? Are they sharing any thoughts, concerns, or "kid stories"?

.   .   .

Stick to your schedule. If you have set aside 15 minutes per confer-ence, stick to it. I remember trying to schedule a 5 minute gap between conferences one year. It didn't work. Each conference just went 5 minutes longer. Remember that parents have schedules, too, and their time is just as valuable as yours. Besides, when schedules aren't followed, other parents hear about it and are less likely to want to attend future conferences.

Look out for your colleagues. At one time in your teaching career, you're probably going to have a tough conference, one in which a parent may be angry and/or have a history of being disagreeable. If a colleague has one of those scheduled, make sure you or someone else is close by just in case. If a parent becomes very loud or threatening, you may want to interrupt if you're comfortable doing so, and ask the parent to calm down or even reschedule. If you're not comfortable doing this, which is certainly understandable, how about asking the principal to do so?

Decide whether students can sit in on their conference. If not, have some books, etc. they can look at while their parents are conferencing with their teacher. By the way, you know there's a good chance they'll be listening to the conversation anyway, if possible. Also, don't be surprised when a parent shows up with your student's siblings, including crying infants.

If a parent states that the available days/times aren't possible, offer a different option outside of the scheduled offerings. How about at the student's home? Dunkin Donuts?

Remember to remain professional, even if you know the parent well or the student is doing an excellent job and you have no concerns.

Watch your language and the image you are projecting, including your appearance.

21

THANKSGIVING

A boy who was always talking about his farm was asked what he was going to eat at Thanksgiving. He replied, "My cat, Salem, lives with the turkeys."

"We all know you can't cook from our Thanksgiving party when you cooked the gross sweet potatoes."

Thanksgiving is an American holiday. At home, we celebrate it by eating a lot and watching football. In school, elementary students celebrate this holiday by eating and doing pilgrim things.

Classroom teachers are faced with a dilemma at this time of year. How Thanksgiving is, or is not, celebrated may be a district decision, a building decision, or it may be up to each grade level or teacher. If it will be celebrated in your classroom, the teacher has quite a bit of planning to do, with one initial question being, will there be food at this celebration?

Classroom Tales…

The most time honored tradition in the elementary classroom is to trace your hand and make a turkey from the outline. Is that still done today?

Most years, my class made things like applesauce to share with classmates. Later on, we began making pies. It helped with our math skills in measuring and, also, working together because the kids were in charge. Luckily, the person who taught home and careers let us use the oven in her classroom because the faculty room oven was heavily booked the day or two before Thanksgiving.

One year, a parent offered to bring in a turkey. We made side dishes and placemats, but that turkey made it seem like we were one big family. It was amazing!

We have a teacher who had a Pilgrim outfit which she wore every Thanksgiving. She looked like the perfect Thanksgiving mom and everyone knew it was her favorite holiday, which I shared that I didn't quite understand. One day around the holiday, she snuck into my room and put up all kinds of Thanksgiving decorations.

…and Lessons Learned

Some think having parent volunteers is more work. I think it's worth it.

I understand how times have changed regarding bringing food items into school. I also recognize that a time crunch for teachers means less time for "fun things" like celebrations. However, the experiences you offer and share with your students are what many will remember most, more than workbooks and lessons. Just remember that Thanksgiving isn't always a happy experience for some kids so if you can find ways to celebrate with your students, please do so.

If you know your students well, it should come as no surprise if students in your class do not celebrate, or even acknowledge, Thanksgiving.

I really emphasized sharing, courtesy, and kindness in my classroom. That included special events like celebrating Thanksgiving. If something didn't turn out the way we hoped, we made do, whether it was a burnt pie, a food item brought in that didn't taste very good, or just not having enough.

WINTER

22

THE REALITIES OF THE HOLIDAY SEASON IN SCHOOL

A third grader compared reindeer and caribou and shared, "I know a big difference between them. Reindeer are magic and can fly, but caribou are boring and just walk."

This time of year is filled with images of big Thanksgiving gatherings with eating, parades, and football, and, for most of us, Christmas, with carols, trees, and presents- think of Chevy Chase and his plans for "the Griswold family Christmas". Unfortunately, the reality for many students is that the holidays don't live up to those lofty expectations.

Classroom Tales...

One of my students called me on the phone one night and sang Christmas carols to me.

. . .

I was on a tour with the principal of a nearby elementary school to gather design ideas when he became mortified upon seeing a manger scene on a classroom door. This was a public school. Santa was ok, but Jesus wasn't.

A parent stopped in to see my principal because I did a Hanukkah presentation for his daughter's class. He seemed to feel that I was spreading Judaism. I suggested he visit my classroom where I had my Christmas tree and lights set up.

One year I bought an artificial tree for my classroom, sort of a nice "Charlie Brown tree". Every December, I'd ask for volunteers to put it together during recess. I really enjoyed just giving them the box and watching them put the tree together as a group.

Two or three of my girls once rewrote the words to the Wassil song and sang it for me. I still have the copy.

My December read aloud book was "The Best Christmas Pageant Ever", by Barbara Robinson. It's the story of the Herdman children, who were troublemakers in school and in the community, and their participation in the church Christmas pageant. As my students listened to the book, there were many discussions about religion and the story of Jesus. I was always a little overmatched on this topic since I grew up in a Jewish home.

Over the years, I did many Hanukkah presentations in classrooms, showing a Menorah and saying a Hanukkah blessing while lighting the candles. My wife, who was brought up in a Catholic home, was also asked to do Hanukkah presentations at her school, which we always found pretty funny (by the way, she did a nice job).

...and Lessons Learned

For many kids, the holiday season is the most difficult time of the year because they don't have that "perfect family" atmosphere. It's not just about presents and food- it's the atmosphere that isn't necessarily filled with happiness. Like with many "problems", you can either ignore this or address it.

I taught in districts that were overwhelmingly Christian so Christmas decorations were acceptable, although I also had Hanukkah decorations. It may appear contradictory, but, although Christmas decorations and trees were common, depictions of Jesus and/or manger scenes were not generally acceptable in public school classrooms.

Be flexible. "Stuff happens" isn't just an expression. Anything associated with the holiday season can be controversial so be ready to adapt. One example from my classroom is that I had kids who didn't celebrate any December holidays so if we had a Christmas party, for example, they couldn't attend. Instead, we held a "mid-year party".

23

SUBSTITUTE TEACHERS

A young student was being asked to identify the letters of the alphabet. She was not having much success with any of the uppercase letters. She was not doing any better with the lowercase letters until she came to the lowercase "f". Then her face brightened and she said that she knew that one. We waited for her to say it was the letter f, but instead, she said, "That's Facebook!"

Although substitute teachers can be found roaming the halls any time of the school year, the holiday season seems to require more subs than some other times. As a teacher who has arranged and planned for subs many times over the years, I can say that it is more work getting ready for a sub than being in the classroom myself. As a retired educator who has worked as a sub, you quickly realize the good, bad, and ugly. The good is that, at the end of the day, you go home- no papers to correct, no plans, phone calls, or meetings. The bad is that you're in someone else's classroom where you don't know where everything is and you're following someone else's plans. The ugly? Students view you as an outsider. You hear a lot of "Mrs. Smith doesn't do it that way" and kids feel the need to test you.

Classroom Tales...

One of my students once ate a sock when I had a substitute teacher in my room. When I asked him why he did this, he said he just wanted to see what the sub would do. By the way, there was a note from the sub. She wasn't coming back.

I was outside at recess with a 5th grade class when one of the kids punched another student in the face. I told him (the puncher) to come over and he promptly ran in the other direction. I had to have the principal come outside- a first for me. I remember thinking to myself- does this kid know who he's dealing with? Then it came to me. He didn't know and he didn't care.

I was working with a small group of first graders in the math teacher's room. At the end of our group time, because we ran a little late, I walked them to the gym, where they were sure their class would be. They were wrong. Then we tried music. Nope. I finally got smart and walked them to the office to check the class schedule and brought them to art.

Back in the days when I had to call my own subs, I would use a sub list for names and numbers. One morning I called a sub and was told by a parent that she had moved to Oklahoma six months ago. I guess my sub list wasn't up to date.

I was subbing for the afternoon and the teacher had set up a video on the Smartboard before she left. It looked interesting and I was curious as to the program so I began fooling around with it. Of course, I lost it.

I was subbing one day in a school where all of that grade's teachers were in a meeting so there were subs in several rooms. They kept coming over to me for help with their Smartboards. That, in itself, is pretty funny.

I was a building principal in a district that paid so little to subs that we often couldn't fill the positions. My first task on many mornings was to walk around my school with a clipboard listing the positions without a sub, including classrooms.

...and Lessons Learned

It sounds obvious, but make sure you have clear, well written plans for subs with plenty to do. I always wrote too much, gave too much background info, and had enough work assigned to last a week. That was extreme, but understand that a sub may get through something in half the amount of time that you thought it would take.

Make sure your students know that if you're ever out the sub is in charge. That may mean that they do some things differently than you do, but they're still in charge. Also, let your kids know that the work assigned that day was planned by you and if there's a problem, they can talk to you when you return.

If you plan on a sub showing a video, using a Smartboard, or any other piece of equipment, I can almost guarantee that either the sub won't know how to use it or the equipment won't work.

· · ·

Always include in your plans the names of at least one or two teachers that your sub can go to with any problems or questions. Most teachers also include the names of a few kids that are especially helpful.

Offer help or just stop in to introduce yourself when there's a substitute nearby. No matter how good the plans are, subs almost always have questions, such as the location of the rest room or faculty room. Stopping in before the kids arrive, as well as during the day, even for a few minutes, shows good will and everyone benefits when a classroom runs smoothly.

24

HOLIDAY PROJECTS IN THE CLASSROOM

My kindergarten class is sitting nice and quietly while doing calendar. Then there's a smell and I try to ignore it until one kid yells out, "Who tooted?" We couldn't ignore it anymore.

Teachers have a balancing act this time of year, making sure their students continue to work hard in math and reading, complete homework assignments, and study for that Friday spelling test, while also doing holiday projects- hopefully with parent volunteers.

My students' parents also played a key role in these projects. I guess they really played two roles. The first was in supplying many of the items we needed in class to complete the projects. The second role parents played was coming into school to provide "hands on" instruction, guidance, and modeling for students. Without parent volunteers, my projects wouldn't have been possible- and they added to a wonderful holiday atmosphere in our classroom!

Classroom Tales...

We made gingerbread houses most years- not because they came out well, as many collapsed under the weight of all of that candy, but because of how much fun they were to make. Parents walked around helping, but mostly to make sure that the kids didn't go overboard sampling the "construction materials".

Making glass ornaments was my favorite activity. They looked great and were simple. Just pour a little paint in and swirl it around, add another color or two, and set it out to drain and dry. Every year, though, at least two kids poured in too much paint because they wanted more colors and ended up throwing out their ornament because it never dried. A couple of them could still be sitting there draining to this day.

Many years I took photos of the kids to be used in ornaments or some other project. The photos I enjoyed most were of each student by our classroom tree wearing reindeer ears- blackmail material for when they get older! Their expressions varied. Many enjoyed posing, but there was always a couple that had that embarrassed look on their faces and just wanted it over.

I'm not sure if it was the hopeless look on my face, but salespeople always flocked to me when I wandered the aisles at our local arts and crafts store hoping for inspiration as I planned holiday projects.

...and Lessons Learned

Leading up to Christmas there is a lot happening in the classroom. In order for these projects and special events to run smoothly, inviting parent volunteers in is a great strategy. Not only does it help to involve parents in their child's education, it helps to make you seem more parent friendly.

It always helps to have a model to show before any project is started. Unfortunately, I was better at showing what would happen if you didn't follow directions.

It can be tough as the teacher because some of your parents are there to volunteer while others are there only to hang around with their kid. Be patient, but also very clear as to parent responsibilities.

It's imperative that you make your expectations clear with students as to how they will respond to parents. My kids knew that many activities wouldn't happen without parent volunteers and they were expected to show them respect.

25

BIRTHDAYS IN SCHOOL

A student gave a teacher a birthday card with "hi" written on the front in small letters. Inside the card it said, I thought you'd like to get a little "hi" on your birthday.

"I'm going to try to come see you very soon. I guess I can't get enough of old Mrs. L.!"

Celebrating birthdays in the classroom was a time honored tradition for me and many of my colleagues. It meant sharing the treat after the "birthday boy/girl" had passed them out, often with the help of a friend or two. This was followed by a rousing chorus of Happy Birthday sung by the class after the honored student chose 4-5 friends (6? 7?) to lead the singing. Of course, after singing Happy Birthday, I always started them singing again with "Are you 1, are you 2...".

Classroom Tales...

I loved the occasional birthday celebration when a parent sent in a cake or brownie tray that wasn't cut up. Then I had to find a knife and decide if the student could do the slicing or if it was up to me.

We celebrated birthdays in school, but sometimes we knew that certain kids weren't going to bring in a treat to share. For one boy, a teacher assistant who knew the family baked cupcakes for him to share with the class.

One third grade student of mine brought in invitations for a party he was having at his house, but he was only inviting some of the kids in our class. He wasn't sure how to hand out the invitations since not everyone was getting one.

One teacher had a husband who always came in around her birthday and made a big breakfast for her and her students. We always knew it was her birthday when we smelled the bacon frying!

A student brought in a treat for his birthday, but forgot that it needed to be kept in the freezer until he would be sharing it. He left the bag with the treat in the classroom and it melted all over.

The best party I ever had occurred when one of my kindergarteners became concerned that children were not having nice birthdays after Hurricane Katrina. Her family was somehow affiliated with a church in Waveland, Mississippi, which was ground zero. This little girl's mother approached me about having a birthday party for the children in the elementary school there. With the help of the Salvation

Army, local businesses, and parents, we collected all sorts of donations for this project, which went on for four months. The culmination was when the two of them went to Waveland for a week, where she went to school in a tent with her new Waveland friends. We skyped with her daily and they delivered all the party supplies for a huge birthday party! They also delivered all the school supplies we collected for the elementary school, which included a suitcase full of gift cards from businesses so they could go to neighboring cities and purchase what they needed. While they were there all the new books arrived that we had collected to restock their library. The finale was a televised simultaneous birthday party between our classroom and all the kindergarteners in Waveland. It was one of the greatest experiences as a teacher that I have ever had!

I guess this came from my Grandmother who always reminded us of her upcoming birthday, but I always reminded the kids about mine. One year they actually threw a party for me. The kids told their parents and they brought in all this stuff to help me celebrate.

A colleague was very upset when one of her students was celebrating a birthday that day in school and the student's father had called to say he was bringing in presents for the child. He also wanted his other children who were in different grades brought to the room so they could enjoy the party.

A new student in our school was celebrating his birthday and Mom and Dad walked right in to celebrate with us. I didn't know that this was common practice at their previous school so it was certainly a surprise to me.

. . .

Before the school year started, I would put together little "birthday recognition" items including a birthday pencil, a treat or two, a book, etc. I hate to admit how often I forgot to give these things out.

Almost every class has students that have a birthday that falls during summer vacation like mine. We always chose a day in the spring to celebrate summer birthdays and included treats and singing. I didn't allow the "Are you 1..." song for me for obvious reasons.

...and Lessons Learned

In my experience, most schools have morning announcements. That's a simple way to recognize students by name for a positive reason and, even though it isn't always "appreciated", announce the birthdays of teachers and other adults who work in the school as well.

Many schools have either limited what food items can be brought in or eliminated them altogether. This may be because of allergies, concerns with peer pressure or parental responses, but, regardless, find a way to recognize that special day for each student.

Take 10 minutes out of the day to sing Happy Birthday and share a snack, like cupcakes, if allowed. For some kids, it may be the only recognition they get.

26

ART, LIBRARY, MUSIC, AND PHYS. ED

"I remember when you did the zipline in gym class. Wow, those were the days!"

Pet Peeve: Glitter. Enough said.

When discussing light and color in art, a student remarked, "A rainbow is more than just colors." Interesting!

As a classroom teacher, I looked forward to my planning time, when my kids were at what we called "specials"- art, gym, library, or music. I corrected papers, got out materials needed for the next lesson, etc. Sometimes, I had a snack or just relaxed from a busy morning. I think it was good for students, also, because they had a chance to get out of the room and work with a different teacher. Perhaps most important, there were always students who excelled in these areas who might not be as interested in the subjects they had with me.

Classroom Tales...

I joined the kids during a unit when they had equipment out like a balance beam, a rope wall, and a zip line. The students loved seeing their teacher on the balance beam and fly across the gym using the zip line. I didn't try to climb up the rope, though.

In addition to often providing materials for specific projects, our art teacher also helped with her expertise. Once, when studying ancient Egypt, she helped us make a life size mummy. Lots of masking tape and newspaper, I seem to recall.

My students in third grade learned how to play the recorder in music and often wanted to play a song for the class. Sometimes, they were pretty good. Other times, not so much.

In our K-5 school, my fifth graders often outgrew the resources we had in our school library, but the middle school librarian let them walk down to use her school's library. The only problem was that they had to walk through the middle school cafeteria. I just told them to be ready to duck.

One particularly large fourth grade girl was very nervous when trying the zipline, which involved stepping off a six foot high ladder while holding on to a small trolley handle. After several attempts at trying this failed, I finally encouraged her to let me hold and spot her. This worked, as long as I held her by the waist which did boost her confidence to attempt this on her own. Her first "solo" ended by her stepping off the ladder, releasing the trolley, and taking me to the ground.

· · ·

I had a gym teacher when I went to elementary school who was tough. Any problems and you got a swift kick in the rear end. That was back in the 60's, though.

Part of the elementary physical education program was swimming for several weeks during their gym times. My job as a classroom teacher was mostly to supervise the locker room, although I usually hung around to watch them in a very different environment. These are some of those memories at the pool:

- Some kids were really uncomfortable changing in front of others so I just told them to change in the bathroom stalls.
- Others were just scared of the pool overall and being forced to go in deep water. I assured them that wouldn't happen and told them that if anyone struggled, I'd jump in to get them- I'd be mad, but I'd do it.
- One day, two parents walked in and sat in the bleachers to watch their child (I invited parents to visit, but asked them to let me know when they would be there). You should have seen the look on the coach's face when he saw adults he didn't know walk right in.
- The boys were ALWAYS ready before the girls.
- Some of the kids were using deodorant for the first time. Some really needed it and some used a lot.
- We had to walk through an unfinished breezeway to another school where the pool was located. There was a roof, but it wasn't enclosed and since it was winter, we froze, especially on the way back when some kids still had wet hair.

...and Lessons Learned

Once in a while, go to specials a little early so you can see them in a different environment. Some who may not be strong readers or writers may be exceptional in art or music. It's good for you to witness these strengths as their teacher and they'll feel great knowing you've seen them excel.

Join your kids in the gym and shoot a couple of baskets. Play the recorder or sing with them in music. Try one of their art projects. Anything you can do where they see <u>you</u> in a different setting, away from the classroom, especially one where you can "play" will never be forgotten.

Make sure to communicate with the teachers in these areas so you know how your students are participating, behaving, etc.

27

BULLYING

ESL kid- "You a funny old woman!"

"If he hits you, hit him back.... Bullies are just looking for attention-ignore her and she'll leave you alone....Tell the teacher....Maybe he just wants to be friends with you....If you stand up to a bully, she'll back down."

Most of us growing up were affected by bullying in some way. Maybe we were bullied, maybe a good friend of ours was a victim of bullying, or maybe we were the bully. Regardless, bullying is one of the most harmful experiences a child in school lives through, and often is remembered well into adulthood.

Classroom Tales...

At dismissal, the class bully came up and slammed my locker shut as I was getting my stuff out to go home- a favorite past time of his. I was so mad, I took this wooden horse I had just finished in shop class and hit him with it, breaking it on him. I then started shoving him and screaming at him all the way down the hall. Teachers were watching this spectacle, knowing that he had to have done something awfully bad for this little kid (I wasn't the tough, macho guy I am now) to be shoving this big bully down the hall, and although he tried to look innocent, I don't think anyone was fooled. That was the last time I ever had trouble with him. The funny thing is, and I know it sounds like a sitcom episode, we became friends in high school.

When I was a principal, there was a parent who stopped in to visit once in a while who liked to brag about the time he put the high school principal up against a wall in his office. He had bullied that administrator and was trying to send me a message as well.

A student from another class approached me about one of my third graders. He said that my student often took money or candy away from him at the end of the day when they were on the bus. The girl he named was always well behaved and never in trouble. Turns out he was telling the truth.

I have two nephews in elementary school who were both victims of bullying. One nephew has alopecia and is completely bald. He got picked on daily. The other has severe stuttering and his classmates were brutal.

When I was a principal, a teacher approached me in tears about a colleague that was pressuring her to join a certain committee. He intimidated her, as he did quite a few others, and she asked for my help in getting him to leave her alone.

.   .   .

I was in 7th grade. There were three girls who were very close friends and there were at least three of us that wanted to be included in that "inner circle". One of the "outsiders" started trying to get the other girls to exclude me by saying things like I was mean or that I bought my clothes from K-Mart. I was so surprised and hurt at first, I didn't know what to do. The other girls were sort of passive, not really joining her, but not defending me either. I made it a point to smile at the girl who was being mean and give her a compliment. The other girls started to see that clearly I was not being mean and they got mad at <u>her</u>. As she quickly lost "social capital" she got angrier and said and did things that made it worse and soon she was in quicksand that she couldn't escape. I remember finding her alone in the hallway and her being really upset. I told her that I forgave her for saying those mean things about me. Then it was over, but she never had the same position in that group again. She now was at the bottom of the pecking order and she remained there the rest of middle school.

In four years of high school, I never used the boys bathroom, not even once. There was too much going on in there and I wanted to avoid those situations.

A teacher in my grade level often intimidated colleagues by confronting them in front of others, both teachers and students. One time in the main office during the school day, she complained loudly about something that she was told I had said. Another time, she loudly voiced her displeasure with me in the faculty room at lunch time over a teacher assistant's schedule set up by the principal.

I was subbing in a fifth grade class that I had been in a number of times and considered a really nice group. When the kids were having a snack, three girls were talking about another student and the clothes she wore. They were convinced that the other student had worn the same clothes for at least two days in a row. A classmate who looked quite sad was sitting alone nearby. Was she the student that the girls were talking about? Is this a form of bullying?

Our school guidance counselor approached me about a meeting she had with some sixth grade students. It seems that the students had shared that three teachers in the grade level were always talking about the fourth teacher and even made faces at her when her back was turned.

In 9th grade, there were several girls in my neighborhood I'd been friends with who just decided to ignore me. They wouldn't talk to me where we lived or even at the bus stop. Although I had other friends at school, this was really difficult because we lived near each other and our parents were friends, too. Even the boys in the neighborhood were in on it and wouldn't talk to me. It was so bad that I would leave late to get to the bus stop so I wouldn't have to stand there in silence while the other kids stood together and talked.

...and Lessons Learned

I have to admit that I don't like specific "bullying prevention programs". It's like designating February as "Black History Month"- what about the rest of the year?

"An Ounce of Prevention is Worth a Pound of Cure"- I think I have that right. On the first day of school, make your expectations clear as to how you expect your students to treat one another and how you will treat them, as well. Enforce these expectations, model these behaviors, and follow up with any problems with parents, administrators, etc. My room was my "island" and I tried my best to make sure that courtesy and respect was the rule- not the exception. In other words, I couldn't control everything that went on outside my door, but I could control what happened inside my room.

That being said, there's probably some form of bullying that goes on in every class, even if it's not the "school yard bully" image of a student physically harming another student. As a teacher, keep your eyes open and make sure your students and parents feel that they can always talk to you. Just remember that bullying can take many forms, with threats and violence just one of them.

Being a good role model as a teacher is one of the most difficult parts of the job. I've known quite a few teachers that followed the philosophy of "do as I say...not as I do". It doesn't work that way and students, even in the younger grades, pick up on the way that teachers treat each other.

28

TEACHERS AND STUDENTS
EXCHANGING GIFTS

"Mrs. B., can I ask you a question?" "Sure, Thomas." "Did you mean to do that to your hair?"

I love to buy gifts for people anyway, so giving gifts to my students was a very enjoyable task for me. It actually began on the first day of school when I presented each student with a book and continued throughout the year with holiday pencils, special treats, and other assorted "goodies".

This time of year, as well as the last week or so in the school year, students often brought in gifts for me as their teacher. Now, truth be told, I enjoyed receiving gifts as much as I did giving them.

Classroom Tales...

Every year, I received at least one or two mugs that had "World's Best Teacher" or something similar. I appreciated the thought, but, quite honestly, how many mugs can you use?

· · ·

I always gave a gift bag to each child with pencils engraved with their name, maybe a candy cane and Hershey kisses wrapped in red or green, a book, of course, and another item or two. They especially liked the candy.

One 5th grade student gave me a Christmas tie. It was made by her Mom and I wore it every year on the last day of school before Christmas. That "little girl" has children of her own now, is a teacher, and joined me for breakfast a few years ago.

I once received an overnight stay at an inn for my wife and myself, which may have been the nicest gift I ever received.

One fifth grade girl gave me a keychain with a purple sneaker attached, similar to what she always wore, while another gave me a board eraser that she brought in after New Years. She was embarrassed that it was late and that it wasn't anything that she considered "special".

I often wrapped gifts to give to my class during our Christmas party. *"Hungry Hungry Hippo"* was a gift from me to my students and it was the loudest game ever. I also gave a new electric pencil sharpener one year- who would've expected such excitement!

Every Christmas at my home, I hang ornaments from former students. One or two still have the names on them, but I have no idea who gave the others. I do know that some of these ornaments are around forty years old.

...and Lessons Learned

This is one of those "do as I say...not as I do". I really stink at writing thank you notes. Don't be like me.

Always try to write student's names on the gifts that they give. You'll appreciate it years later when you try to remember who gave you that Christmas ornament.

This may not be necessary to say, but you will receive a wide variety of gifts over the years. Like many adults, your students are not always confident in the gifts they are giving you, especially since quite a few are chosen by their parents. You absolutely must be equally appreciative of every gift, regardless of it's value.

Scholastic Book Club always has special offers to take advantage of to buy class sets of books for the holidays.

Some schools or specific teachers have eliminated the gifts that students give to teachers and, instead, encourage charitable giving. I really like this idea. I also really like getting presents. Sorry.

Most important are the lessons to be taught here. Opening gifts in front of your students is a wonderful opportunity to show thanks, humility, and appreciation for the time spent together each day and the gifts they were kind enough to present to you. It was also a time to model how you appreciated the opportunity to be their teacher whether there was a gift...or not.

29

PRINCIPAL'S RESPONSIBILITIES

"Mr. Principal, did anybody see your veins pop out of your neck and steam come out of your ears yet?"

"It must be interesting to have the power over everything that happens in a whole school."

I was an elementary principal for five years. There were aspects of that job that I absolutely loved, like being able to visit all of the classrooms in the school and see the great things teachers and kids were doing. There were also things about being a principal that I didn't like, such as the paperwork.

For most students, as well as teachers and parents, the principal is the person in charge. Other district administrators, including the superintendent and school board members, just aren't as familiar to those individuals in a school as the principal. So, the obvious question then becomes...what does the principal do every day? How does he/she spend their time? How do they ensure that the teaching and learning are first rate?

Classroom Tales...

I worked with a principal once who didn't seem to be comfortable visiting classrooms. As teachers, we always said that the fastest way to get him to leave your room was to ask him to join your class or help a student.

As a principal, I once had the brilliant idea of cleaning out the faculty room over a vacation when the teachers were away. Our head custodian and I removed a couple of old copiers, threw away junk that had been stored there, hung curtains, etc. It looked great! When the teachers came back, the only person I heard from was a teacher who was angry that something she used had been tossed.

One principal believed in managing by wandering around. She didn't enter rooms except to open the door and say good morning. Usually the door closed before we could respond.

I worked with two principals who amazed me by how they appeared to know the name of every child in the school. It didn't matter how the student performed academically or how they behaved, they just knew every kid by name. Me? Not so much.

I once dressed as a chicken and walked around clucking all day as a reading reward. I also dressed in a big hoop skirt with a wig and makeup when I "danced" with a local ballet company performing "The Nutcracker".

Dealing with angry parents is part of the job, also. There was a food fight in our cafeteria and I had all of the fifth graders involved pick up everything from the floor. I had three calls at home that night. The first was from a Dad who was told by his ex-wife to find out what had happened that day, although he sounded disinterested. The second was from a very angry Mom who began screaming and then, when I said that if she wanted to continue the conversation she should call me in school the next day, began swearing. The third was from a Mom who had no problem with students picking everything off of the floor except that they should have been wearing gloves- she was a nurse. I thanked her for her idea.

There was a grade level in which there was a clear divide between three teachers who were approaching retirement and two teachers who were ten year veterans. One of the more senior teachers told me one time that she felt I favored the "young ones".

...and Lessons Learned

When you are hired as a principal, you can not, and should not, be part of the "gang". You gave that up when you became an administrator. You can be friendly with the people you supervise, but there is a line. Don't cross it.

Being a principal also means playing "politics" to an extent. There are deals made, battles to sometimes be fought, and others ignored even if you think they are worth fighting. Get used to it. I never did.

Try very hard to be fair and objective with everyone. As I stated above, others may not view you as fair, but do your best. Try very hard to show no favoritism.

· · ·

Like all jobs, there will be some parts of being a principal that you will really dislike. Get over it and do what you have to do.

I've always said that fifty percent of being a school principal is being a good person. Even if you know very little about teaching and children, be fair, honest, pleasant, and courteous with both the adults and children you work with and you'll be ok.

30

CHEATING

"Throughout the year, you were always there giving us advice, helping us with problems- everything."

I was pretty strict when it came to my students doing their own work. Being dishonest, such as in lying or cheating, was a "pet peeve" of mine mentioned the first day of school. It was reinforced often, and included encouraging my kids to simply do their best. I also reminded them that they wouldn't really learn anything if they cheated, and that no one would trust them, etc. Regardless, it could be a difficult battle.

Cheating in school comes in many forms, including copying answers from a classmate's paper, not doing your fair share when working in a group, turning in someone else's work, etc. There are two aspects related to cheating that make it a difficult area to address. First, teachers have to impress upon students that cheating is wrong even though kids witness cheating on a daily basis in areas as diverse as sports and politics. Second, teachers are often faced with the dilemma of suspecting a student of cheating, but not being positive as to what actually occurred.

Classroom Tales...

One student in third grade tried to hide the spelling words under her leg during the Friday test.

One student brought in math homework that had been written by her babysitter. She told me that, although the babysitter wrote the answers, she told her what to write.

A friend who usually did poorly on spelling tests wrote out the words ahead of time and turned in that paper as his test. The teacher changed the order of the words and really let him have it.

...and Lessons Learned

If I suspected cheating, I'd talk to the student(s) privately and ask the standard question, "If you were the teacher, what would you be thinking if you saw students talking to each other or looking around during a test?"

Encourage your students to do their own work by leaving space between desks, especially during tests. I always described this as giving each student privacy and also so their neighbor wasn't tempted, rather than to stop cheating.

Especially in this day and age when testing seems to be such a priority, let students know that you just want them to do their best and nothing would be gained from cheating. Feeling that kind of pressure at the age of seven felt unacceptable to me.

If you do believe a child is cheating and subtle comments haven't helped, you may choose to contact parents. If you do, beginning the conversation with "we have a problem and this is what seems to be happening" is more effective than beginning with "your kid cheated".

31

THE SCHOOL NURSE

A kindergarten student, when I asked her group if they were ready to work hard, said, "I'm going to do a good job because my meds are working really good today!"

The school nurse is sometimes the most popular person in an elementary school. Kids in those grades often want to go see the nurse to share how they feel, what hurts, and why they can't stay in class. He/she is almost viewed as a type of social worker or counselor, someone to talk to, and whose office provides a safe haven, free of work, directions, and relationships with both peers and teachers. Going to the nurse's office is like taking a time out from the day.

Teachers, on the other hand, play a balancing game, trying to decide if their student really needs to visit the nurse or just needs a little sympathy. It's a dilemma. By the way, there are many times during the school year when teachers visit the nurse because of their own ailments.

Classroom Tales...

I was subbing when a little girl came up to tell me that she was really feeling sick to her stomach so I sent her to the school nurse. After a little while, she came back, explaining that the nurse told her to return to class, but the student fell in the hallway and hurt her knee. She wanted to go back to the nurse.

As a principal in a small rural district, if our nurse was out, the Junior/Senior High nurse from across the street would come over. If she was out, I was the third string nurse. I "played this part" several times. I was ok giving out band aides and calling home, but the sight of blood is another story. We won't even talk about a student throwing up.

One student was sent to the nurse because of an asthma attack, and it was so bad an ambulance was called. The parents were mad because they said it was just for attention. It happened again while she was in school and she ended up in the hospital, with oxygen levels so low that a nurse said if she didn't get there, she might not have survived. The parents took their child out of school and sent her to live with her aunt.

I can't tell you how many times I sent a kid to the nurse holding a garbage pail because they either did throw up or thought they were about to, or holding tissues on their nose because of a nose bleed.

A kindergarten class had lice for months and became "regulars" in the nurse's office.

.   .   .

My son was sent to the school nurse once when he seemed a little groggy in the cafeteria. After arriving at the nurse's office and sitting for a few minutes, he slipped off the chair in the midst of a seizure. That's when, as a parent, you truly appreciate having a health care professional, the school nurse, available for your child.

One day I was putting my school bag and lunch in the passenger side and I managed to hit myself in the head as I closed the car door. I had a gash on the side of my head and I kept wiping the blood away until I got to school and went to see the nurse.

For field trips and special events like field days, the nurse would pack a first aid kit for teachers to bring with them. I don't know about the legalities of this practice, but I carried a lot of inhalers, meds, and EpiPens for my kids.

...and Lessons Learned

I don't know if vomiting (throwing up, puking, etc.) is appropriate for this topic, but I can pretty much guarantee that it will happen at one point. Hopefully, if your student feels as if this is imminent, they can make it to the nurse. Having them take a garbage can helps because it at least gives them a "target" if they need one. I always sent a friend along any time a student needed the nurse anyway- it's actually a good way to build up the helper's self confidence as they walked a classmate down the hall. *Make sure you get the garbage can back- they can be worth their weight in gold.

You have to decide almost daily whether to send a child to the nurse or not. Ideally, you will make that decision based on the needs of the student. Realistically, though, you have to remember that we live in a time of litigation and social media.

. . .

Just as your students need to learn what the school nurse can or cannot do, you need to remember that she is not your personal physician. Many educators, myself included, visited the nurse when we had certain symptoms before coming to school or that seemed to develop during the day. Sometimes, we might have wanted a break, too.

Make sure you find out if the school nurse provides anything for your classroom, such as band-aids, tissues, etc. If not, those items may need to go on your summer school supplies list for parents or you had better head to the store yourself.

If one of your kids is at the nurse's office, stop in and see them when you have a break even if it's only for a minute or two. They'll really appreciate it and remember that you care.

Be prepared when you get a phone call from the nurse that your student who isn't feeling well is going home. Often, you won't have a lot of time to get all of their things together, like their jacket, homework, books they need, etc.

32

DRESS CODES FOR KIDS AND ADULTS

A fourth grader was showing me his tee shirt and remarked how his Dad took one look at it before school and said, "What the heck is that?" The student then explained how he changed Dad's words a little.

Of all of the issues facing teachers and students, I've always felt that determining dress codes was one of the most difficult to establish and enforce. Rules in this area are usually too subjective and kids, as well as adults, are more likely to rebel against this rule. Parents often react negatively to the consequences given to their child and teachers are likely to make it a union issue if pushed.

Classroom Tales...

There was a girl in 5th grade who was about ten going on sixteen, as the expression goes, both in the way she dressed and the makeup she used. I remember sending her to the bathroom to wash her face one day when she had really overdone the makeup and suggested she have her parents call me if they had any concerns. They didn't because she wasn't applying all that makeup until she got to school.

I had a student who wore a hat with a beer emblem that had to be removed and another wore a sweatshirt with a snake wrapped around a nude girl. That one had to come off, too.

In my elementary school, if I wanted to wear jeans on a Friday, I had to put a dollar in a can although I don't remember what the money was used for.

When I was a kid, I had school clothes and play clothes. Other than the possibility of getting teased if your pants were too short or if you had a bad haircut, I don't remember there being any issues with how we looked.

I know a principal who sent out a memo to teachers saying jeans were no longer allowed. I'm sure you're not surprised when I say that almost every teacher wore jeans the next day.

One Halloween, I was called over by colleagues to see the costume one of our teachers was wearing. To be honest, it was really inappropriate for school.

Because I was often the only male teacher, if a boy was wearing a tie for school pictures or some other event, his teacher would often send him to me for help with the tie.

· · ·

My first year teaching, I taught in three different schools. In one class-room, it was always hot and humid so I usually didn't wear a tie. The principal in another school called me over one morning to where he was standing with some other teachers, one of whom was wearing a tie, and loudly proclaimed that this is the way teachers are supposed to dress.

...and Lessons Learned

When a student is doing their work, completing homework assign-ments, has a great attitude towards school, and is courteous to others-do you really want to focus on what they wear? Maybe you do, if their clothing is that much of a distraction or is inappropriate in some way.

Dress codes for teachers are just as difficult to establish and enforce as those for students. A dress code for teachers doesn't mean that jeans aren't allowed or males have to wear a tie. It's just that if you're regulating how students dress, then you must make sure faculty members have certain standards, too.

Personally, I always felt that working out problems or concerns with students and parents was much more effective than simply having a rigid code when it comes to issues like student dress. Then again, I was an elementary person and things may be quite different in secondary school.

As a teacher, even the clothes you wear can send a message. On the first day of school I usually wore a colorful tie with kids on it. Students also liked my Garfield Halloween tie and my Grinch tie at Christmas. When I wore an occasional pink shirt, kids usually asked me about it, which gave me the chance to address stereotypes.

.   .   .

Looking professional is very important, but different positions call for different expectations. I've never seen a gym or art teacher wear a tie, skirt, etc.

33

CLASSROOM GIFT EXCHANGE

"Miss P., are you married?" Miss P.: "No, but hopefully someday." Student: "Do you have a boyfriend?" Miss P.: "No." Student: "Uh oh."

Every year that I taught, my students took part in a gift exchange with their classmates. I organized this in a number of different ways in my classroom, including exchanging toys or books. There were years when each child brought in an item labeled whether it was for a boy or a girl, and other times, each student picked a name of a classmate out of a container so they knew who to buy a gift for. As the gifts came in, they were placed under our class Christmas tree until the day when we would open them and have our party.

Personally, I loved just sitting back after everything was opened and watching the kids play or read their new books. I appreciated the thoughtfulness they demonstrated (some more than others) and the opportunity for my students to just be kids. That was the way I wanted to end the day and that was the way I wanted to begin Christmas vacation.

Classroom Tales...

I worked with a teacher who held a different type of gift exchange. When it was time to open the gifts, each child had the option of choosing an unopened gift from the pile or they could choose a gift that someone else had chosen and already opened. A note to parents had explained all of this beforehand and it had been explained in class. Still, tears and angry phone calls were the result, and I decided right then that I would never do this type of gift exchange.

When I was probably around ten, my Mom got a gift for me to use in a grab bag. It was a jigsaw puzzle with 1,000 pieces and nobody wanted it. I mean no one. I was absolutely embarrassed then and still remember it to this day.

A couple of times when we did a book exchange, a student brought in a used book from home that was in bad shape or was really inappropriate for the grade.

Sometimes I had each child bring in a gift without their name on it, but labeled "for a boy" or "for a girl". The idea was for kids not to know the specific person who brought in the gift. Looking back, the whole"boy/girl" thing was sexist.

I had a pretty low spending limit so parents wouldn't see this as a burden, but one student came in with a gift that was at least triple the suggested amount.

A few days before our gift exchange and party, a boy approached me one morning to say he had forgotten who he had picked.

...and Lessons Learned

I learned from other teachers to always have a few extra gifts wrapped and ready to go just in case. The kids who forgot to bring in a gift to give were just as appreciative as those who received those gifts.

The success of your classroom gift exchange is measured by the response you see in students. Are they having fun? Do they seem to appreciate the gift or did they at least acknowledge it? Were your kids comfortable with what they brought in for a classmate? If the answer to these questions is yes, you did a good job.

When the date for the exchange drew near, I contacted parents whose child hadn't brought in their gift to see if there were any issues with the exchange. Sometimes they simply forgot and sometimes they just hadn't sent in the gift yet. Other times, though, a parent shared that money was just too tight, and it was then that I would assure them that it would be taken care of. This is where having established relationships with parents since the beginning of the year really helped.

Always give guidelines as to the expected cost of a gift. I usually said that $5 was the maximum to be spent. Some went over and some spent quite a bit less, but it seemed to be just right.

Consider a book exchange. Other than the obvious reasons, like encouraging reading, there are other advantages, also. Although toys are fun, a lot of kids have plenty of toys already and parents will often say that their child doesn't need more. Cost is another factor, simply because many kids books aren't that expensive.

34

LEAST FAVORITE TEACHER

On the last day of school one year, as all of the teachers were on the sidewalk waving to students as the buses were leaving, the teacher next to me turned and said, "Well, another year shot to hell!"

Earlier, I included a chapter entitled "My Favorite Teacher", where I asked about a favorite teacher you or your child may have had, or a teacher you admired as a colleague. Today, I'm going in the opposite direction.

Although I've always believed in emphasizing the positive and focusing on good experiences, we also tend to remember the bad situations we face in school. Many of us may have had a teacher who just wasn't the right "fit". Discipline, different personalities, or motivational methods used- for whatever reason, it just wasn't a good match.

Classroom Tales...

In elementary school, our music teacher asked each student to sing a solo as part of our quarterly grade. One student with a speech problem sang "Little Red Caboose" and the class burst out laughing. When she called my name, I just sat there looking down. This happened at the end of each quarter with this same student singing "Little Red Caboose", which led to laughter, and then to me sitting in silence when my name was called. The teacher tried failing me one quarter and gave me an "A" another hoping to find what would motivate me to sing. I don't remember her ever asking me why I wouldn't sing, although I'm not sure I would have answered her anyway. To this day, though, I rarely sing in front of people.

A nun loved my brother. He would write a short paragraph and get an "A". I would write a full page with documentation and get a "C". My father was tired of my complaining and went to open house, where the nun told him that my brother had a lovely smile. He came home and told me not to worry.

In eighth grade, the teacher had us pass our homework forward each day at the start of class. One day, as she glanced at the papers, she noticed I forgot the date so she handed it back to me and said to put it on her desk when I had filled it in. Less than a minute later, I walked up to do as she had asked. At that moment, she saw me and, for whatever reason, thought I was trying to turn in the assignment late. She yelled at me and then hit me really hard against the side of the head.

The art teacher came to our room once a week...the worst day of school for me. Every week we had to draw one of the students as they stood in front of the room. I could not draw people, but I was great at barns, trees and flowers! So one day my mind wandered to the hill outside of our room. I created what I thought was a brilliant drawing. She came to my desk and tore up my drawing, giving me an F for the day. Then, in front of the class she began yelling until I started crying. I was a good girl, and this was very hard on me. From that day on, I never signed up for art from 6th grade to high school. I can see the day in my mind even 50 years later. I was so scared I became sick on art days. I have many grandchildren now and I love to sit with them coloring barns, trees and flowers! My drawings to this day are brilliant!

I had played clarinet for quite a few years in elementary and middle school, took private lessons from "Mr. C" for $2 an hour, and was actually pretty good. When making up my schedule for ninth grade, I was asked if I wanted to be in band. Since I had decided to switch to a different instrument, I said that band would be a possibility in a year or two after I learned to play my new instrument. Well, my first day in high school I was scheduled for band, so I walked up to the teacher to explain that my schedule was wrong, but he just told me to sit down. I tried seeing him the next 2-3 days and he would just tell me to return to my seat. The end result is that I spent the year in band, blowing as loud as I could, and that included marching band.

I was told by my third grade daughter's teacher that she was one of a handful of kids that were very bright so they were going to teach themselves. The teacher had too many "low" kids to take time out for the bright ones. The following year, the same teacher had my son and called the second day to say he was too talkative. Then she proceeded to tell me what was wrong with every child in her class and that it was going to be a difficult year. Two months into the school year, my son is holding on to the bannister, sobbing, and saying, "don't make me go to school- don't make me be in her class!" Heartbreaking.

. . .

In 5th grade, I had Mrs. K. After a lesson on nouns and verbs we had a worksheet to do identifying them in sentences, but I guess I didn't understand the difference between them because Mrs. K. just screamed at me and told everyone in the world that I got every single one wrong. She then dragged me into the hallway and started shoving me against the wall. I can't remember what she was saying because I was terrified. I do remember my head hitting the wall several times. When she was finished, she walked back in with me and the class must have heard everything because they all looked so scared. Every day after that I faked being sick when it came time to do English lessons in Mrs. K.'s class.

My least favorite teacher? Hmmm, we all have them. There is the big, burly, female gym coach who put a lifesaver around my waist, made me climb up the diving board steps (a real diving board used in swim meets) and yanked the rope when I refused to jump. There was the middle school gym coach (male) who made a point of letting me know that he was surprised that I was chosen in the top quarter of kids when we played games. When I asked why, he stated that there were a lot of other kids more popular than me that were chosen later in the game. That was a self-esteem booster! My least favorite teacher of all was a high school English teacher. She would tell the class, repeatedly, how her own children were in college at Dartmouth and Princeton. Fast forward to year twelve. She thought it would be fun to go around and ask each one of us where we'd be going to college. A few kids were not going at all so you can imagine her reaction to that. When it got to me, I proudly announced that I would be going to Cortland for teaching. As quickly as the words exited my mouth, her comment was uttered. "Oh..(with a look)... a STATE school, how lovely." I will never forget those words.

...and Lessons Learned

Although most of us had many positive school experiences as kids, anyone who has had a bad experience remembers that also, and sometimes those bad experiences have had a lasting affect on us well into adulthood. Do the best you can when teaching in subject areas such as reading and math, but make absolutely sure you treat each child with kindness and understanding.

Listen to your students. If you have built positive relationships with them since the first day of school, they'll let you know in their own way if they have a problem or they know of a classmate who does. As a teacher, I was no pushover. I had high expectations of them as students and as individuals, but I believe they saw me as caring and kind.

Sometimes, as adults, we view some issues with kids as so minor that we just ignore them or give them the "just get over it" speech. Try to remember that those "little things" aren't little to them.

35

CLASSROOM MANAGEMENT/DISCIPLINE

"One thing I liked about you is that you didn't yell at us."

There have been countless books and articles published on classroom management and/or discipline. I believe that's because there are so many factors involved and strategies to consider for a teacher. Still, I felt the need to share just a few "tales and lessons" from the classroom. I even struggled with the naming of this chapter because, to many teachers, parents, and students, classroom management really refers to classroom discipline. In reality, they're different simply because the better your management is, the less traditional discipline you need. By the way, I'm sure it won't come as much of a surprise when I say that teachers, also, respond to rewards and consequences like everyone else.

Classroom Tales...

We once had kids working in teams to put together projects on different countries. Other classes voted on the best project and I took the "winners" to McDonald's for lunch. We had a great time except for the student who dropped fries between the front seats. I'd find the occasional fry months later.

A second grade teacher had a fishbowl and a paper fish for each student. If the student misbehaved, his/her fish was taken out of the tank and the offending student was told that, oops, their fish had died.

I had a 5th grade student many years ago who had a very difficult time with the art teacher. The young man was always disruptive, and it took away from the class when he battled back and forth with the teacher, who would then send him to the principal, where he would often sit for 1-2 hours. Consequences didn't matter to him. We changed his schedule around so he had his music instrumental lesson during art. He'd come back to the classroom after his lesson and we'd then walk down to the art room- slowly.

A colleague once taped a kid to his seat.

A boy from another state moved to our school and was placed in the class next to mine with a first year teacher. He was in trouble constantly, hitting classmates, taking things, and breaking every rule there was. A meeting was scheduled and I was asked to attend, I thought because of my knowledge and past experiences as a special education teacher. Instead, he was placed in my class for a few weeks until he was to be moved to a special education setting. I still remember walking with my class down the hall when the student in question jumped on the back of a classmate who kept walking while I peeled the young boy off him.

There was a teacher I worked with who had a big refrigerator box in her room. She used it as a "time out " space for kids who weren't behaving.

I taught a third grade boy who had been disruptive in class for several years. His family life was very difficult, having been given up by his parents and living with relatives until they also moved away without him. I hadn't seen him in quite a few years when this tall person with long shaggy hair and wearing a long coat came walking into my classroom one day. After the initial shock wore off, it was a wonderful surprise!

A teacher in my grade level had a very difficult time with student behavior. This same teacher rarely left her desk when teaching.

... and Lessons Learned

You'll notice that most of the stories shared reflect negative behavior. The reality is that the vast majority of your interactions with students will be positive. It's just that we tend to remember the bad behaviors more.

When we hear the term "discipline", we often think of students misbehaving and punishments given. In reality, "classroom management" is more accurate and begins with the first day of school with rules and expectations made clear.

It's so easy to "threaten" to give certain consequences, but take a breath before you do. Just like being a parent, once you give a consequence, it may be hard to take it back (no electronics for six months, for example). The difference with being a teacher is you don't control everything with your students. There may be a school policy about recess or homework that doesn't work with a consequence you want to give.

There is that expression, "you catch more bees with honey". Keep things positive with your students by giving out more compliments, rewards, and other examples of praise instead of resorting to negative responses right away.

Remember that you work with colleagues. Rewards and consequences you set up are often compared to those in other classrooms. Be mindful of this, especially with those in your same grade level or similar programs.

Regardless of whether you have a chalkboard, a markerboard, a Smartboard, etc. get students up there to use it. They're not going to hurt it, they love to go up there (mostly), and they'll pay attention more. In other words, the more involved kids are in their learning, the less time you'll need to devote to discipline.

Move away from your desk and walk around your room. Your "presence" close by may be your best management tool.

Classroom rules, as well as school-wide rules, should be worded positively. Keep your hands and feet to yourself sounds better than don't hit another student, and include a "catch all" rule, such as "behave like a responsible third grader".

36

SNOW DAYS

"Mrs. G., I guess the groundhog was right! He is a smart animal. Do you think the groundhog went back into the hole because he knew we were going to have a snow day?"

An almost unheard of "pet peeve": "Two hour delays throw off my routine."

I retired from teaching a number of years ago, but I still get excited on a snowy morning seeing the names of school districts closed or opening an hour or two late. I hope that excitement never goes away!

Like so many other occurrences during the school year, though, snow days are not nearly as simple as most children think they are. Just making the decision itself is tough because it's based on factors such as changing weather conditions, what neighboring districts do, and available days in the school calendar. Imagine being a parent who has to arrange day care for children who won't be going to school that day. Teachers have to rearrange their plans because they will have a shorter academic week, so lessons are changed, tests may be postponed, etc.

As complicated as snow days may be, the words that strike fear in the hearts of every parent and administrator are "school is closing early". This is truly when problems multiply. Dismissal is a mess because buses often can't load at the same time and parents aren't home for their kids, don't show up to pick up their kids because they aren't aware of the announcement, or they simply can't leave work.

Classroom Tales...

More than once my wife would share that my school was closing after I was already in the shower.

A young student was dropped off in front of the school by a parent who then drove off, not realizing that school was closed because of a snow day.

I found out that school was closed when I was already awake and ready. I felt like I wasted valuable sleep time so I got back into my pjs, unmade my bed, and went back to sleep.

We were supposed to get some bad weather, but nothing happened. Six o'clock came along and my alarm went off so I got up, went about my routine, showered, and made my bed. As I was about to head downstairs, I jumped on facebook to see what was happening in the world and I saw that we were closed.

I worked at a school that had schedules set up for one or two hour delays. We didn't use them often, but when we did, rarely were we all following the same schedule.

. . .

The best feeling was when they closed school the night before. It was great to click on facebook and see all of the posts about the closing.

As a kindergarten teacher, most of my students don't know what a snow day is and that we can actually have a day off from school because of snow.

Since I had a long drive to get to school I left my house pretty early. Because it was snowing one morning, I left very early and didn't find out that we had a delay until I got to school and the transportation supervisor and the vice principal were the only people there. A little while later, school was cancelled altogether.

Snow days! Last week we all knew we'd get Wednesday off but the kids could NOT stop talking about snow day myths. Put a spoon under your pillow. Flush an ice cube down the toilet. PJs inside out - you name it, they listed it, and I couldn't get a word in edgewise! So I interjected and told them that I heard you should spin around 98 times before you get into bed. They instantly stopped talking and looked at me like I was crazy, but I got to move on with my lesson. I hope some of them tried it!

As a kid, snow days meant a day on the farm with my cousins and grandparents. It was the best. There were two enormous hills for sliding so we spent the day riding our sleds, toboggans, or pieces of cardboard. Cardboard is the best by the way. Sometimes my grandparents had nine of us there at a time. We literally stayed out most of the day. We were not babies about the cold. We built great jumps in the middle of the hill and almost broke our backs with each try. Of course, then we made the next run a little higher.

As a teacher I lived for snow days and unexpected time with my family. It was nice to have the same snow days as my girls so we could play all day, but it was sometimes nice to get a snow day when they didn't have one so my wife and I could be alone. There were also days we drove to school and risked life and limb and could never figure why the superintendent didn't call the day. There was always a buzz around school about what an idiot the superintendent must be.

I think I love snow days as much as my kids do. It takes me back to my childhood when my mother would open my door and tell me that school was closed. I would be snug in my bed when I heard the snow plow go by. Now my kids and I have a routine. First, they sleep in and everyone stays in their jammies for a long time. During the day, I cook a nice hot meal like soup or chili and I bake. I always have to bake on a snow day. At some point the kids go out to play in the snow and if it's the right kind of snow they build a snow man. Eventually, they have to help their dad shovel snow. Their nicknames are "snow removal units 1 and 2". We love our snow days!

Snow days- forget about the kids, the anticipation of teachers for a snow day is amazing! I know that I immediately start thinking about the possibility of a snow day whenever the weather report suggested it and what it meant to my schedule. Will I be missing a tough day, a difficult group, or a meeting?

As a parent, I loved snow days. It was just such a good feeling to let them sleep in. When they were little, they loved to play in the snow. A snow day just seemed like an extra gift. I also liked that I didn't have to worry about them being out in nasty weather either getting to school or getting home from school. The kids and I just wanted to have the day to do what we wanted. We watched some movies or played some games. My husband always felt like snow days were an extra gift to fill the day up with jobs and chores and didn't want to waste a minute. Not always a good fit for those of us wanting to laze around.

...and Lessons Learned

Strongly encourage your students to complete any homework, studying, etc. even if bad weather is in the forecast. Remind them that you never know what the weather will be.

Teachers, also, should not assume that there will be a snow day. Plans, progress reports due, etc. have to be completed regardless of the weather report. Don't forget that usual bed time, either. As I reread this, I realize I sound like Bah Humbug.

If it's snowing during the school day, the gossip concerning an early dismissal will start early and continue throughout the school day. Much of this gossip will originate with teachers.

Seeing the kids two times a week makes it very hard to deal with snow days. I either extend the unit, or power pack the next lesson.

I'm convinced that deciding whether to have a delay, a full snow day, or to remain open in bad weather is one of the worst aspects of being a superintendent. No matter what you do, fifty percent of the people in the district think you're an idiot.

37

RACE IN SCHOOL

If you could be Abe Lincoln or George Washington, who would you be? "I would be Abe Lincoln because I want to be taller than everyone else and he got rid of slavery and slavery was bad." Another student: "I would be George Washington because I'd like to powder my hair and ride a horse."

I've always felt that being a good role model was an extremely important part of teaching, but that can be very difficult for teachers because of different backgrounds and experiences, including views regarding a person's color, religion, etc. For our use here, I want to concentrate on the relationships between black and white students.

Two notes here: First, my experiences as a teacher reflect that I worked in rural schools for my entire career, which were overwhelmingly made up of white children and adults. Second, quite a few of the stories included here were from others and I thought it was important to include them because they presented experiences that needed sharing and, in these cases, I did very little editing.

Classroom Tales...

When we filled out the BEDS forms each year (school data), those of us who worked in the office could easily name each of the African American students in our entire school. It was a short list.

My parents had strong views concerning race (sadly), but that's how it was. We were forbidden to have black friends. I am happy to say that my children seem not to notice color, race, special needs, or any other differences. Having said that, none of them have close friends who are black. I think I was always more concerned about raising them to be compassionate and to treat kids the way they would like to be treated. Race wasn't an issue. Hmmm, why don't they have close friends who are black?

I went in to say good night to my oldest when he was in kindergarten. He was holding two of his toy soldiers and smacking them together as if they were fighting. I asked what he was doing and he said they didn't like each other because one was black and the other was white, and that's what they talked about in school. I don't think he really got the message.

When I was in high school, there seemed to be a great divide between black and white students. Based on color, kids sat at different tables in the lunch room and rumor had it that the players on our basketball team didn't pass the ball to teammates of a different race.

I went to school and there was one black student in our whole population. We all thought it was quite cool, in part, because she had a huge Afro and she put special stuff in it. I was in the drama club with her and she let me bounce my hands off her hair. It felt different from mine.

Every once in a while one of my elementary students would come up to me to say that a classmate had used "the N word". Sometimes it was handled privately, and sometimes it became a class discussion.

My children were seldom exposed to black people when they were young because the area we lived in and our small circle of friends never included blacks- only because there were no blacks we even knew. When my oldest daughter went to kindergarten, her teacher was a wonderful black woman. Her skin color was no issue for my daughter, who couldn't wait to go to school. She loved her teacher! So, when my next daughter was ready for school, we requested the same teacher. Another excellent year! When it was time for my son to start, we made the same request. When my son and I went in for summer orientation, he was so excited...especially to have Mrs. T. like the girls did. To my great embarrassment, we walked into the room and the first thing out of his mouth when he saw her was, "I want a white teacher!" Why, I'll never know, but he went on to have a wonderful year and loved her just as much. I'm still perplexed to this day where that feeling came from.

While teaching, I had a few different ethnicities in my classroom over the years. I used it as a great learning opportunity. Right at the beginning of the year or whenever they entered my class, I started a discussion about race and color. I made it perfectly clear that we were all different in some sort of way and we should accept everyone for who they were. One related project we did was separating the children by hair color and making them stay in a certain part of the classroom. I made sure everyone understood this was only a demonstration but blondes were treated differently from brunettes and so on. By the end of the day, the kids had had enough and understood what it meant to be segregated. The best story I have was a kindergartener going home and telling his parents he was white and couldn't use the drinking fountain or bathroom all day. I got an irate phone call from the parents over that one.

My best friend since kindergarten is black- we only had two black families in the school and racism wasn't an issue. We marched in a St. Patrick's Day parade in NYC when we were in high school and the band and color guard stopped for lunch at a McDonald's. While we were waiting in line, I remember an older gentleman standing there who turned and said "When did they start allowing N (the "N" word) in here?". We just stopped and were stunned because we had never heard that term (and we were in high school) being used to describe one of our own... and then chaos erupted. People started yelling at him. I was just trying to get to T. to somehow protect her and get her away from him and what was happening. In 38 years of friendship, it is one of the few times I have seen my friend cry. She said the word didn't hurt, it was the fact that he had singled her out and made her feel less than the rest of us. Who has the right to do that to someone?

I started my instruction designed for Black History Month by asking kids to name famous black Americans. They only knew professional athletes, singers, television or movie stars, etc.- no scientists, politicians (other than Barack Obama, who was elected towards the end of my career), authors, inventors, or military leaders. Students did know Dr. Martin Luther King, Jr. because we have his birthday off in January. In order to learn about African Americans that were not athletes or movie stars, I would bring in biographies for students to choose from. By the way, Dr. King wasn't a choice, as he was the "go to" guy in many classrooms. Truth be told, I didn't know quite a few of the subjects in the biographies I made available, such as Mae Jemison and Madame C.J.Walker. I'm not sure what this says.

. . .

When I went off to college, due to the uniqueness of my name, my roommate thought I was black. Her upbringing, along with our other suite mates, was much different than mine, and my potentially being black was a concern. Well, wouldn't you know C. (my best friend who is black) was with me and was the first one across the doorway, bringing in my stuff. She turned and yelled to my parents, "Mom and Dad, in here, this is the room!" My roommate, her family, and my suite mates couldn't see my parents in the hall. In came two very decidedly white people with a black girl calling them mom and dad... there was a lot of confusion until I arrived in the room! But I do have to say, by the end of college, C. and I had taught them that color makes no difference in a person's character, or lack there of.

...and Lessons Learned

It certainly isn't fair, but in many schools where there might be a very small number of students of a particular race, that student represents everyone of that race simply because of the limited exposure the majority might have. In the schools where I taught, there were very few African American kids, so for the majority of students who were white, that single black kid represented every black kid.

Teachers need to put personal prejudices and generalizations aside when teaching as much as possible. This isn't easy and actually impossible for some.

It's my belief that a month designated as Black History Month is not as effective as a teacher providing ongoing and integrated instruction in this area throughout the year. To put it simply, if the only time you mention African Americans in a historical context is in February, you have a problem.

. . .

Once again, if you teach in a community that is overwhelmingly
white, that can be an issue because you may find yourself gearing
instruction to students who have no experience or understanding of
those who are of a different race. As a girl in college once said to me,
upon learning that I grew up in a Jewish home, "So, you're a Jew? I
never met one before."

38

VALENTINE'S DAY

"Mrs. T., I will never, ever forget you."

V alentine's Day, especially in elementary school, can be one of the most enjoyable, yet stressful, school days for everyone. For kids, there are questions about who to give a Valentine to, what it means, which cards to choose, and filling them out in time. For teachers, it's another school day when kid's minds are elsewhere, you have to respond to those with hurt feelings, there may be a party to arrange, and you probably have to come up with yet another project to plan. All of that being said, I really enjoyed Valentine's Day when I was teaching.

Classroom Tales...

Like most holidays in school, I gave each student a gift bag. For Valentine's Day, I included a book, a pencil, and a couple of pieces of candy. It was kind of depressing if any of these things were left on the floor, but it was worse if a pencil was found because I usually had each student's name printed on them.

There were quite a few projects done in classrooms to hold Valentines. The best I saw was a covered wagon, which I never considered because of my lack of artistic talent. I often had kids cut out a big heart, trace it to make another, and then staple the two together leaving the top open for Valentines before decorating it. I always showed them a model that someone had made (maybe my wife) correctly and one with the top stapled together by mistake- that one was mine.

Some teachers sent home a note to parents requiring their child to give a card to every classmate, but I never did. I just pointed out to my students that every pack of cards came with more than enough and there was just no reason to hurt someone's feelings by not giving them one. I also added that a Valentine didn't exactly mean you were getting married.

One parent wrote to me and wanted to know when Valentine's Day became another Halloween since every Valentine came with a piece of candy.

For the last ten years or so I brought in approximately thirty to forty carnations wrapped separately which would be given to any adult in school that worked with my students. This included the other teachers in my grade level, special area teachers in art, speech, gym, music, library, special education, the secretary, cafeteria workers, etc. The best part was I had students deliver the flowers and explain to the recipient that it was a thank you from our class. Truthfully, we gave some flowers to people I wasn't really fond of, but that wasn't really the point.

When my timing was good, we wrapped up our Valentine's Day party just before dismissal. One year, when kids were getting in line to leave our room, I reminded them to take home any treats that were left over. As the words, "and be careful with any bags of candy that are already opened" were coming out of my mouth, one of the girls grabbed her bag of candy, not realizing that the top was open, and candy flew all over the room.

I really enjoyed choosing the Valentines that I would give out each year. They were usually Harry Potter or some other "cool" subject- at least, I thought they were cool.

Every year there was a student who gave out Valentines, but forgot to sign them.

As a kindergarten teacher I found Valentine's Day to be the most difficult holiday of any we celebrated. I am pretty sure it was the mystery of the box and what they would find in it. I insisted that everyone make a valentine for everyone in the class. I also made the parents create the Valentine's mailboxes as a family project. The best part for my kindergarten students was having their "5th grade friends" coming to help the children deliver their valentines and then having them come back to help their friend to read all those valentines and share in our party snacks.

...and Lessons Learned

I know it's obvious, but holidays and other special events go a lot better if you plan well in advance. I made sure to have plenty of red, pink, and white construction paper on hand. If I wanted "ready to assemble" projects, I used Oriental Trading Company. The quality was ok, but I used them because all of the parts were there, directions were included, and they were affordable. AC Moore was my favorite "brick and mortar" store to go to for class project materials because they had everything and the people who worked there could help me with anything I needed- very important for a person like me with limited ability.

Make it easy on parents and your students. Send home a class list so the kids won't have to remember every classmate's name. This also serves as a follow up to your message about kindness for all.

Having individual students deliver a flower to a teacher or staff person is seen as a pleasant distraction- no one I knew ever objected to a flower being delivered as a Happy Valentine's gift from our class. That being said, students often asked if they could go around school during our party because they had Valentine's for other teachers, etc. Not every adult in school enjoys disruptions like this and some really resent it.

One of the reasons I enjoyed holidays like this is because I had very specific rules. The kids knew when the party would start and that we would have a normal day until that time with our usual work. That meant that sharing and opening Valentines had to wait until the party. They also knew that anyone who didn't follow this rule would miss at least some of the party and that I was not a teacher who "bluffed". Yes, I did have a student or two who missed some party time over the years.

SPRING

39

PERFORMANCES, PLAYS, AND AFTER SCHOOL ACTIVITIES

Teacher: "Does anyone know who Susan B. Anthony is?"
    Student 1: "Wasn't she on the Golden Girls?"
    Teacher: "That's Bea Arthur."
    Student 1: humming the theme song to The Golden Girls
    Student 2: "Mr. T., thanks for being our friend."

In most elementary schools, students get their first taste of performing in front of an audience, whether it be in a class play or concert. It's great because it doesn't usually require a major time commitment outside of school, yet it allows children to experience speaking, singing, playing an instrument, or acting. The downside is that these activities still take time out of busy schedules, whether it is a class using time during the school day to rehearse or specific individuals missing class time to prepare for an upcoming concert.

Other than school activities, students are often involved with sports, scouts, or hobbies that do not involve their school "careers" at all. You may hear about them often, and they may be looking for your support.

Classroom Tales...

I had a seat in the front row at a school concert, right in the middle, so I could get a good view of my kids and they could see me, also. Big mistake. Our music teacher was directing and there was very little room between where she was standing and where I was sitting. If you've attended school concerts, the music teacher directing is often quite animated in his/her motions and this particular teacher was moving so much that I spent most of the concert trying to shift my legs away from her and brace myself just in case she fell on me.

Another third grade teacher and I decided to have our classes put on a play together. We chose a very difficult musical that included thirteen songs in approximately 6 languages in addition to multiple speaking parts. They did great, even though we made a very poor choice.

When I was a principal, our district's drama department performed "Peter Pan" and used quite a few of my elementary students in roles. This meant lots of rehearsal time both during the school day and after hours. The performances were wonderful and well received, but what I remember most was my being a "flyer", along with the Superintendent and the local mayor. As flyers, we were responsible for pulling the ropes that enabled the main characters to fly across the stage. The first rehearsal didn't go quite as planned, although the Mayor did well. The Superintendent cut himself on the cable and I fell off my bucket (I was too short to get my character high enough, so I had to stand on a bucket) when I started to pull my rope, fell to the floor, and couldn't move because I couldn't let go of the rope since my character was flying through the air. We got better the next practice.

. . .

During school concerts and rehearsals, students often had to sit or stand on risers (similar to bleachers) for rather long stretches of time. I remember one student fainting while standing and another vomiting. I think that both of these occurrences happened during rehearsals.

Another teacher and I were invited by our students to a dinner recognizing their achievements in an organization they were a part of. It was an evening event, and it meant a long drive back to the school community we taught in, but I think they really appreciated us being there. Besides, I seem to recall I enjoyed the food.

During a performance we were putting on for parents, one of our students was speaking when his Mom stood up to take a photo. He burst out laughing and couldn't stop until she sat down. When she tried to take his photo again, the same thing happened. Memorable!

My wife and I attended two recitals that my students were performing in. One was a dance recital that took hours in a very hot auditorium. I remember that we had to stay until the end because of the way my kids were scheduled. The other was a piano recital at a university in the area in which a very gifted student of mine was the featured performer. She was amazing and is now teaching her own children how to play.

...and Lessons Learned

I always told my students to be very patient with their music teachers the day of a concert because those teachers were probably very tense.

. . .

Regardless of whether you're a classroom teacher putting on a play or a music teacher having students perform in a concert, surprises are going to occur. Be ready and be flexible.

As a classroom teacher, it's difficult to give up the time it takes to prepare for a concert or performance. Keep in mind, however, that these experiences may be the ones kids get more from and remember as they get older. Like hands-on activities, kids will remember these lessons more than workbook page 56.

We all have a life outside the classroom, but if possible, try to attend events that your students are involved in outside of school. This can be an evening concert or play, but it can also be a baseball game, a dinner recognizing club accomplishments, etc. They'll appreciate it and will likely remember it for years!

40

STANDARDIZED TESTING

"I got on Honor Roll first quarter, but this quarter I got a "C" in math. I know, I know, I should do better!"

I f you're as old as I am, you may remember the "Californias" or the "Iowas". I seem to recall that these were standardized tests we took back then. I guess that was where the tests came from and I have no idea what they were used for, or by whom. If my Mom got a copy of my results, I'm pretty sure she didn't share them with me. Later on, as a teacher, we gave our fifth graders the New York State Writing Test. We'd get the results back and adjust our instruction accordingly. That, I thought, was why we had standardized tests in the first place. Before I retired from teaching, the standardized tests we were giving had grown in number and in the ways they were used and perceived. In my opinion, there are now priorities other than improvements in instruction.

Classroom Tales...

A teacher in a room next to mine had two or three boys who generally put forth very little effort. On a testing day, they completed an essay in less than fifteen minutes, while most students took two-three hours. She wasn't happy.

One second grader in our school was such a wreck during testing that she had to leave the classroom. Her mother explained that she had been studying non-stop so she would do well.

One year the principal had me ask another teacher for a sample essay question to practice with my special education students. The day of the test came and there was the exact same question we had already done as a practice test.

There were certain guarantees when you gave a standardized test to students. The first was a conversation as to what a #2 pencil was. Second was that some kid wasn't going to fill in the circles all of the way and another would take five minutes to make sure each circle was perfect. Finally, a student was going to answer a question out of order so all of the rest of the answers were off by one.

I had a fifth grade boy who really hated to write. It turned out, though, that he was great at recognizing strengths and weaknesses in writing pieces done by classmates. He improved in his own writing over time and did quite well on standardized tests he took at the end of the year.

.   .   .

One essay topic in a standardized test seemed to suggest a scary response, which kids loved. Unfortunately, most went way off topic writing a gory story and bombed.

After emphasizing the importance of these tests as we practiced for months, when the scores came in, we were told by the principal that we couldn't share the results with students.

Our students wrote essays which were then scored by district teachers. Our scores across the board were quite low until we realized that the scorers prioritized spelling and grammar over content, even though that went against the scoring rubrics they were supposedly using.

...and Lessons Learned

The good news is that Standardized Test results can help teachers and administrators make adjustments in instruction. The bad news is that these test results can, and have been used, as a "weapon".

Kids reacted in many different ways to testing. I always felt I needed to be a "coach", knowing which students needed to be prodded to do their best and which ones needed me to help them relax. Do we really see value in rising stress levels in kids who are seven or eight years old?

I'm convinced that if all you ever do as a teacher is practice for upcoming standardized tests with workbooks, your kids will probably do very well, but they will learn nothing, while possibly hating school.

41

FIELD TRIPS

I was having a discussion about trains and asked if any students had ever been on one. Some students raised their hands and I asked one of them where he went. He told me, "I'm right here!"

Field trips served many purposes for students, including celebrating the end of the school year, curriculum tie-ins, and visiting places many students would not be likely to visit otherwise. I loved taking my students on field trips, although there was quite a bit of planning, beginning with where you were going. I always thought the best part of a field trip was seeing students outside of the classroom environment, interacting in different ways with classmates and chaperones.

I suppose I was fortunate in that I went on field trips as a teacher, principal, and parent, each playing a different role when it came to responsibilities. I'm a bit of a control freak, so I wanted every detail finalized and confirmed, with backup plans, "just in case".

Classroom Tales...

Our grade went to a festival of nations on an extremely hot day. I remember two things. The first was how a student and parent wanted nothing to do with an African themed display. The second is that we ran out of water and I was walking across the field hoping to find some for our students at one of the refreshment booths and not really being able to feel my body moving.

We took our third graders on a boat trip down the Hudson River. Pardon my ignorance, but the man selling refreshments on the boat asked me if he could offer Red Bull to the kids and I had no idea what it was. When he explained, the answer was no.

To raise money for our class trip to Boston, we sold candy bars one year and made more than enough. Kids would take home cases of different kinds and sell to family members, other kids, and even door to door.

One way we raised money was holding movie nights. First, my class voted on what movie we wanted to show, not an easy task for kids with lots of opinions. The night of the movie, we hung a big sheet on a wall in the cafeteria and showed the movie to kids and their families, many of whom were in pajamas. I think we charged $1 per person and we made as much from snacks as we did from admissions.

To raise money for a field trip, we hosted a roller skating night at a nearby rink. It was lots of fun and I think the kids enjoyed seeing me skate, too, although I needed about three kids to help me up when we did the limbo and I fell. I still believe the fix was in when they lowered the bar when it was my turn.

We took our 5th graders to a planetarium and when the lights went out during the show, kids starting calling out and one threw a shoe. I felt pretty helpless.

Once, we held a "Teen Time" for elementary students, modeled after an activity our middle school did. We had the pool open, volleyball, basketball, and other games, and one area set up with pinball machines and air hockey. The kids loved it, but even though parents were told to sign their children in and come in to pick them up, we still had "drop offs" and others who got a ride with another family. It was a bit of a zoo- thank goodness we had lots of parent volunteers.

Students were really buzzing when they heard one of the teachers using some pretty vulgar language when she was stuck in a bathroom stall on a field trip to Montreal.

We took our kids to the Bronx Zoo even though quite a few parents were scared at the idea of going to the Bronx. That also happened when we went to Boston and even on a trip to Albany, NY. If you know how big Albany is, you'd understand.

I had planned a field trip for all fifth graders to visit a historical village several hours away. Unfortunately, I wasn't able to go because my wife and I were expecting our second child right at that time. The kids had a lot of fun, but it was a very long day and the other teachers reminded me for years that I didn't go.

·   ·   ·

I know a teacher that did an overnight trip with her class. It sounded like a great idea, but it turns out that when the class arrived in the city they were visiting, everyone went their separate ways until they left the next day.

It seemed wrong to me to allow movies to be shown on the bus, but I finally gave in. Boy, did it make the trip go faster.

When I was a parent chaperone, we went to Boston. When we were getting ready to leave, I was called to the front of the bus and asked if I knew the way out of the city. I really didn't.

...and Lessons Learned

Field trips are a great time to include parent volunteers. Without them, most trips aren't manageable, and, besides, parents enjoy these opportunities.

As the teacher, you're in charge. Make sure students know what is expected of them and that includes how they interact with parent chaperones. I also let parent chaperones know that I was in charge and would speak to them if there was a problem, such as inappropriate language, smoking, etc.

In choosing a field trip destination, it's tempting to focus on places that are just for fun, but you still should go somewhere with educational value as well, and always remember that you're still the teacher when on one.

42

RECESS

Teacher: "What's a dedication?" Student answers "constipation".

I loved recess as a kid and I also enjoyed it as a teacher. It was a chance for my students to burn off energy, get away from having to listen to teachers constantly, and play with friends who may not even be in their class.

You would think that recess would be simple, at least in the elementary grades. Simply bring students outside and let them play. Other than the occasional skinned knee, what's the big deal? As it turns out, recess may be one of the most complicated issues in school.

Classroom Tales...

I was teaching 5th grade when a new student joined our grade. We were at recess and she had been in our school for only a day or two when she fell off the back of the swing she was on, breaking both of her arms. What a welcome!

. . .

While teaching kindergarten in London, two very proper little ladies in my class took up a bad habit of digging in the dirt on the playground and then peeing in it.

When I was in elementary school the girls would huddle in a corner near the building and the boys would take turns running into them. The girls squealed and then the next boy would do the same. I don't really understand it, but I remember it.

I loved recess!! I would get together with all my girlfriends and we would make up dances and then offer to go to all the classrooms to show the teachers.

I heard a child comforting another as they walked in from recess past my classroom. I went out to check and one student had blood streaming from his nose while the little girl with him held her hands below to catch the blood.

I went to a Catholic school which didn't have any playground at all. We just ran around or played kickball. One day some boys were playing "crack the whip" on the ice and plowed me over. I hit my head when I fell so I went to tell the nun in charge, expecting sympathy, not to mention medical attention. What I got was, "well then, stay out of their way".

One of the gyms was open so we would take our kids there for indoor recess on bad weather days. Some just talked or shot baskets, but quite a few played kickball. The only downside is that the high ceiling had nails sticking through. We popped a lot of kickballs during those games.

. . .

My fourth graders squeeze every possible second out of their 20 precious minutes of recess. They form kickball teams and other activities without uttering a word to each other. I watch them from my classroom and find myself wondering...why can't they get their math books out that quickly?

With a hill right next to our school, we'd get the sleds out at recess time. The kids loved it and the only negative was we had to keep an eye out for snowmobilers who would sometimes ride on school property and come flying over the top of the hill.

I like to occasionally bring out candy and will sometimes share with students. A group of fourth graders were playing basketball and I told them I would give them a sour patch kid if they made the shot. They made a lot of shots.

When I was in fifth grade, the boys would get together to play softball every day. Unfortunately, we spent most of recess arguing about batting order, etc.

I remember recess when I went to Catholic elementary school. We played in a fenced-in black top area. Usually the girls played "Four Square" and the boys played catch with a football. Inevitably the football game would encroach on the four square area and the chasing would begin. I can only imagine what the people passing by must have thought when they saw girls in their plaid uniforms, skirts, and saddle shoes chasing boys in their grey dress pants, shirts, and ties!

. . .

My students, who generally aren't very good time tellers at the beginning of third grade, quickly learn what the clock looks like when it is time for recess. They never fail to remind me.

Our fields are still wet from the snow and rain, as well as the playground, so the kids played in the bus circle. The nurse came to me complaining because so many kids were coming into her office injured, She said I should talk to the lunch aides who were not doing their jobs because they were allowing the kids to run.

When I was in kindergarten all of the playground equipment was on top of a bed of gray pebbles. I was running around and tripped over the wooden edge of the playground and onto the pebbles, I remember I was wearing a dress and stockings and I had to go to the doctor's office multiple times after this incident to get all of the dirt out of that cut. To this day, I have a scar over the top of the piece of nylon still stuck in my thigh.

There was a boy who was held back twice in elementary school and we used to live for what he would do on the playground. One time, he got his tongue stuck to the swing set pole in the middle of winter and another time, he flipped out of the swing because he went so high that the chains buckled and he landed on his head. For some reason, though, he never seemed to get hurt.

...and Lessons Learned

I know there are increasing pressures regarding time, test results, etc., but recess just has to happen. Educators have to ensure that the "fun" parts of school, including recess, aren't lost.

. . .

Recess was often used as both a reward and a consequence. Teachers loved having it later in the day when that day's behavior and work, as well as last night's homework, could be determining factors. Besides, everyone was tired at that point.

It's during recess that kids form friendships, develop social skills such as compromise and leadership, and ultimately come back to the classroom ready to focus and learn. It also allows me, as a teacher, to observe my students interact with their peers. Who is a leader? Who is a follower? And most importantly...which of my students are uncomfortable initiating play, have trouble getting along in a less structured environment, or are so painfully shy that they hang out with me, the teacher, for the entire recess.

At least once during the year, join your kids at recess. Play a game, take a few shots, or go on the swings. They'll never forget it.

Check to see if the gym is available when your class or grade is scheduled to have recess. We had many days when we couldn't go outside and a large open space like the gym was perfect to let the kids release some of their energy.

I always made sure there were quite a few games for my students to play on indoor recess days. Some were my own kid's games they no longer used, while others were bought at garage sales or were presents I gave the class at Christmas time.

Please don't make tv watching an option during indoor recess.

. . .

Recess gives kids the opportunity to be exposed to things like team play and camaraderie. It also exposes them to things like acceptance, rejection, teasing, bullying, etc. Not all of these things are good, but they are all necessary parts of growing up. They learn that not all things are fair in life. They learn that they have to try harder at some things than others do. They learn to win and lose- very important. They learn to stand on their own. They learn to stick up for themselves as well as others. They learn that they can disagree and still play together. They learn compromise. They learn trust. They make and break bonds that can't be made in a classroom environment. They learn to think for themselves.

43

TEACHER EVALUATIONS

*Teacher: "How do we make changes in society if we all think differently
and we all think we are right?"*

*Student: "I know what I believe, but I also know that society has to
change. Sometimes, we might not like the changes, but society is ready for
them."*

*"Dear Mr. S., It's almost Mother's Day. Are you thinking about a present
for your mother? I hope so."*

M ost of us want some kind of feedback as to how we're doing
in our jobs. Of course, we hope for, and may even expect,
that we'll be judged as doing a good job, but we can usually accept
constructive criticism if deemed fair and private.

Teachers are no different. We expect to be evaluated and hope or
expect that we will be presented with a positive review. The problems
that exist for this process include the difficulty measuring teacher
effectiveness and then how to address issues. Teachers don't build a
"thing", nor do they have set goals, such as in sales. One summer, I

had a job building chairs. It was easy to evaluate me just by counting the number of chairs I built each day. Teaching is different because students differ in so many ways and have such different needs. Performances of teachers are, therefore, influenced by many factors, so evaluating them fairly is difficult, not to mention that some feel that the results should be made public.

Classroom Tales...

The very first time I was up for tenure, neither of the two principals I worked with (I was teaching in two buildings at the time) had done even a single observation and written evaluation of me in three years. One even asked me to write my own and she would sign it.

I sat in on an observation being done by a building principal in a special education classroom when an upset student ran out the door. The flustered teacher began explaining how this wasn't her fault instead of going after the student.

One supervisor of mine wrote in my observation that he didn't like the color of the marker I had used during the lesson.

In a school I taught in, unless an administrator saw serious problems with a tenured teacher's performance, those teachers had several options as to how they were evaluated, including peer observations, working in a specific curriculum area, etc. Quite a few chose a standard clinical observation because it was just simpler.

I subbed more than once for teachers taking a day off to write the reports needed for their evaluation.

.   .   .

Whenever my colleague had an observation coming up, she got hives.

I knew a teacher who was in a mentoring relationship with a new teacher. Although the interactions were supposedly confidential, the mentor shared the details with just about everyone.

... and Lessons Learned

The purpose of an evaluation is to recognize strengths and recommend how to address weaknesses. The idea is to help the person be the best teacher they can be. Many policies regarding teacher evaluation forget that.

If the evaluation process includes so much paperwork and time spent that teachers and/or principals are missing contact time with students, that's a problem. That means that the administrator isn't in the halls, isn't visiting classrooms, and isn't providing leadership. Most importantly, it also means teachers are missing time with their students.

44

CLASSROOM DISTRACTIONS

Kids in a class needed partners and there was one kid who was misbehaving. The teacher asked for a volunteer to be his partner to help keep him under control and focused. A girl stood up, raised her hand, and said in a perfect voice, "I volunteer as tribute!" This is lost if you haven't seen/read "The Hunger Games", but it's awesome if you know what I am referring to.

I often say that teaching is about the "little things" that happen each day. How teachers react to those little things is pivotal in maintaining an effective classroom. Distractions such as coming back to school after a vacation, the first snowfall of the year, fire alarms going off, assemblies- there are too many distractions to list that disrupt your school day. Try continuing a lesson when a bee flies around the room. How about when you're reading aloud to your class and a child throws up, or the phone rings in the middle of a test because a student is being picked up unexpectedly and a parent needs the child and their homework for the night.

Classroom Tales...

My 3rd graders were taking a math test so the room was nice and quiet. I was taking a box down that was on a high shelf when I lost my grip and it fell on me, with the contents then spilling onto the floor. The kids looked up because of the noise, I assured them that I was ok, and they went back to doing their test. I'm still not sure if that was good classroom management on my part or they weren't worried about me getting hit on the head with the box.

I was doing an observation of a first year teacher one day when it started snowing for the first time that winter. She tried valiantly to keep her first graders focused, but it wasn't working so she told them all they could go to the window to watch for a few minutes until it was time to get back to work. Brilliant!

My class was outside for physical education one day when the fire alarm went off and they had to line up while the rest of the school filed outside to get in lines and take attendance. Because of the drill, they missed most of gym class. To make matters worse, three or four of my students said some very unpleasant things about the principal because of the drill, who then suspended them.

There were many times that the phone would ring in my classroom and I have to admit that it really bothered me. It would often be a reminder of some sort that I forgot to do something, like send a student to the nurse, etc.

During a construction project a tractor was being operated outside our classroom window. Between the noise and seeing this large machine, you can forget about focussing on the lesson.

...and Lessons Learned

All distractions just can't be avoided, but a principal has an obligation to protect "teaching time" as much as possible.

Fire drills and announcements will always occur at the worst possible time during the day, such as in the middle of a test.

Effective teachers just roll with the punches and know when to just accept distractions as part of the job.

45

EXPERIENCING AND SHARING BAD NEWS IN SCHOOL

Sorry, no quote for this chapter.

We all experience difficult events in life, but being a teacher means that you'll not only go through these experiences on a personal level, but sometimes, depending on the circumstances, with your students.

I've often said to new teachers that if you teach for a long enough time, you're going to lose a kid, maybe not in the year that the student was in your class, but at some point. The passing away of a student's family member or someone working in your school are also possibilities, or the difficult events may be something not quite as tragic, such as a car accident, house fire, serious illness, etc.

Classroom Tales...

There was a new teacher assistant who worked with my third grade students. She also always came down to help out when she had free time or after school so my students and I came to know her quite well. In the spring, she became ill and missed the last few months of the school year. Over the summer she was in the hospital and passed away in the fall.

I read in the paper that a young man had been killed nearby when struck by a car. He was from the school district where I taught earlier in my career, and his name sounded familiar, but I wasn't quite sure. The more I thought about it, the more I realized that he was, indeed, a student of mine and he was in my first fifth grade class. That class was memorable to me because seven of those kids had families that split up during this particular school year. One was this young man's.

I was fortunate, I suppose, in that none of my students were lost during the year I was their teacher. However, one committed suicide several years later and another passed away from MS, not to mention the wakes and funerals for the family members of my students and colleagues over the years.

A mom of a 3rd grader in my school and a 9th grader in the high school passed away yesterday morning from cancer. Dad had come in to the office and picked up his daughter the day before so she could say goodbye to Mom in the hospital. Yesterday, he stopped by and shared that he had no idea what he was going to do. Needless to say we were all in tears.

A student who I really got to know well was in jail when he was a young adult and then committed a murder while there.

...and Lessons Learned

If you can't handle a situation, don't be afraid to say you need help yourself. Regardless of the severity, not everyone is capable of dealing with difficult events such as these.

As much as possible when an incident like the ones mentioned above occurs, try to be steady and consistent. In other words, remember that you may be the only one kids can depend on. Sorry for placing that burden on you, but it's true.

I hate to say this, but in my experience, adults in school gossip as much as anyone. Because of this, administrators must share whatever information they deem appropriate, but also make it clear to faculty members what information should or should not be shared with others, especially students and parents. Speaking of which, kids gossip, too, but they also listen and observe adults so information that shouldn't be shared with them is often picked up in bits and pieces.

Imagine how difficult it would be to share news like this with children. To sit down in front of a class to share that a classmate or teacher had died is heartbreaking, and probably requires the kind of training possessed by a school counselor, nurse or other mental health professional.

46

PARENT REQUESTS

During a vocabulary lesson, a teacher showed picture cards, one of which was a garden hoe. One little boy then says, "Well, why does my Daddy call my Mommy a hoe?"

There are many issues when class lists are being formed for the following school year. Who is it that determines the make up of each class? If you're a parent, who determines who will be in the same class as your child and who will be his/her teacher? Most important for many parents is whether they will have a say in their child's placement for the following year.

Many school districts accept parent requests, sometimes because it's a tradition, and sometimes because it's seen as a way of including parents in the decisions regarding their child's education. It's hard to argue with these reasons because most educators support having their students' parents involved in some way. The question then is whether a parent request is absolute, or if there are any shared guidelines for parents in the role they play in determining their child's teacher.

Classroom Tales...

Just about every parent wanted their child to have Mr. H. as their child's kindergarten teacher so almost everyone requested him. The opposite of Mr. H. was Mrs. T. She had developed a bad reputation in the community and not only did she get few requests from parents, but parents specifically stated that they did not want their child in Mrs. T's class.

There was a parent who had a long history of nasty comments and notes bashing teachers. Mrs. L. loved the word "sucks" in describing her kid's teachers each year. She would stop in to see me often and we developed a good relationship. That spring, when I described the process I would be using regarding parent requests I explained how "some parents" just liked to be nasty and insulting and I would ignore those requests. She ended up writing the most positive letter regarding teachers she had ever written. Not one "sucks"!

On the first day of school, a parent of one of my new students told me that she had requested a different teacher, but would "see how it goes".

I was an intern in charge of class lists in a district where parent requests were not accepted. A teacher approached me about her own child, wanting her son placed with a certain teacher. After the principal reiterated that requests weren't allowed, I explained this to the teacher, but she persisted and then went to the principal, who then explained to me that we had to "take care of our own".

· · ·

A teacher I knew was often requested by parents so when another teacher was requested instead, he seemed offended and dismissed this as a "personal issue".

I worked with a principal who encouraged parents to share who they did not want for their child's teacher.

... and Lessons Learned

I worked as a principal in a school district where parent requests were an accepted practice. To make this process as clear and concise as possible, I followed the following steps:

1. A letter was sent to parents several weeks before the class list process would begin stating that if a parent or guardian wanted to share any information that would help us place their child, it would have to be in writing, in the same courteous fashion they would expect from us, and by the stated deadline. It also made clear that the final decision was up to school personnel.

2. As letters came in, the key points were shared with the present classroom teacher and that teacher was asked to share with me any hesitation as to why the request shouldn't be followed in case I was contacted by an unhappy parent.

3. Finally, the classroom teachers at each grade level, already aware of parent requests that had been made, would put their current students together in classes balanced by gender, ability, behavioral issues, etc. I promised teachers that I would contact them before making any changes to the lists they had put together, which rarely happened.

Did this process work? To an extent, yes. It cleaned up the process so parents and teachers knew what was expected of them. Parents felt they had a say in their child's teacher and teachers knew that school personnel had the final say. This eliminated "hallway requests", last minute phone calls, and parents using the opportunity to bash teachers they didn't like for one reason or another.

I believe that schools, if there is a choice, should absolutely <u>not</u> accept parental requests because of the following:

1. Parents often make requests based on rumors, assumptions, or past experiences with a teacher.
2. Each child is different, so just because an older child had a particular experience with a teacher doesn't mean the same will be true of a sibling.
3. There may be reasons why a teacher would prefer not to have a particular student, such as they may be neighbors, related to a student, have had a difficult relationship with the family, etc.
4. Teachers and administrators are the professionals. They are the individuals who need to make the best decisions regarding the educational program and they need to place children in the best learning environment. It's their job.

If your district accepts requests from parents, ego is often involved. We all like to be thought of in a positive way so it can be difficult when you know that another teacher was preferred instead of you. It's easy for me to say not to take it personally, but the truth is that it bothered me when it happened.

47

FORMING CLASS LISTS

"Thanks to you I will probably be the best fourth grader out there!"

U sually in the spring, sometimes in the summer, class lists are
formed for the following school year. The process begins with
who is going to make up the lists, and continues with contributing
factors such as student ability, behavior, social skills, gender, and
special needs to be considered.

Even if there is a clear process as to the formation of class lists,
school personnel still need to determine when lists will be released
and how the information is shared. Then, there is still the matter of
changes. What happens if a teacher retires or budgetary issues affect
the number of sections in a grade level? What about new students
that move into the district?

Classroom Tales...

At my school, we had a system in place where teachers at a particular
grade level got together to build classes of their current students for

the following year. I thought this worked well until a teacher told me afterwards that a special area teacher had come in and "dictated" where all of her students should be placed.

After class lists were formed, the sharing of those lists was planned for a later date, with teachers being directed to not share that information until the appropriate time. One teacher brought her current students around and introduced them to the teacher they would have the following year.

At a school I taught at, we had rankings in place for each of our students, from one through four, in areas such as subject matter, social skills, etc. Then, the teachers at a particular grade level built balanced classes for the following year. It seemed like a smart way of doing things, but the principal often changed students around anyway.

... and Lessons Learned

I believe that classroom teachers should make up class lists for the following year simply because they know students best. That certainly includes academic strengths and weaknesses, but also social skills, family characteristics, peer relationships, etc.

That being said, things happen between the time lists are made public and the start of the next school year, such as new kids being registered. If changes are made to the original lists, the teachers involved should be notified immediately.

· · ·

This may be difficult, but educators need to have a backbone regarding student placements. Administrators and teachers are the professionals and have the most information regarding students.

48

A TEACHER'S CLASSROOM SUPPLY LIST

The question, what would you do if you were president, produced responses such as these: "I'd live in the White House and have a pet monkey and lion." "Every Friday would be pizza day." "I'd walk around and make people pick up litter." "I would make sure every Mom had one day off a week to drink their Mom juice."

S ometime in the spring, months before the next school year starts, there will be ads promoting Back-to-School sales. I know it seems crazy to be even thinking about the next year for your school age children, but it's going to happen and, although parents make other contributions to classrooms during the school year, it's the purchasing of school supplies from the teacher's list that carries the most weight in the classroom. I constructed my list so individual students would have what they needed for school, with other items included to address general classroom needs. For example, pencils and markers were kept by each student for their own use, while boxes of tissues and white notebook paper were stored together as more of a classroom supply.

Classroom Tales...

This may seem like a silly item to ask for, but tissues were on my list for the last number of my teaching years. When I began teaching, the nurse's office supplied boxes of tissues, but that stopped later on. I then began asking each parent to send in two boxes and we often ran out before the end of the school year. By the way, we sometimes had students come in with boxes that were already opened.

Another weird item to ask for were baby wipes, which I used to clean my marker board. They worked pretty well (and smelled good) and when each student brought in a container, that gave me enough for about two years.

I don't remember much of what I had to bring to school when I was a child except for 1 item. My Mom always bought me these really cool PaperMate pens, which were pretty classy.

When I was in stores like Target, I could sometimes hear angry parents voicing their "displeasure" with things that teachers had asked students to bring in. Usually, their complaints were related to costs and sometimes it was about a specific item. I usually walked away without saying anything.

I also asked for whiteboard markers because I used them constantly (this is pre-smart board). I had kids up at the board all of the time, which they loved, and I always thought it was funny how they took a few seconds to choose the color they would use.

. . .

The first time I saw a teacher include plastic "shoe boxes" on their list I was surprised, but each student kept their personal supplies in one, with the shoe box stored in their cubby. When the class cleaned out their desks and cubbies every week or two, there was always this dash to throw all of the loose things into their shoe boxes.

... and Lessons Learned

It's tempting to add all kind of things to your list that you can't order for one reason or another, or that you don't want to have to pay for yourself, but please put yourself in a parent's position. Many have trouble enough paying the bills without an extra long list of school supplies they have to purchase.

Most teachers I knew had certain preferences for specific items like a particular style of notebook or brand of crayon. As the teacher, you may have very good reasons for asking for that item, but, again, put yourself in the parent's shoes and don't expect them to shop at five stores or buy the most expensive brand or type of an item.

I tried to make my list a little shorter every year- something to think about.

If you're lucky, you won't run out of some items by the end of the year and can remove them from your list. In some cases, just storing so much is a problem. I always seemed to have quite a few packages of notebook paper left over each year.

49

TEACHER'S BUDGET

When doing a math problem using ducks, the focus is lost. "What color are the ducks?" Have you been to a farm?" "I like ducks, but horses are better."

Most years I had a pretty good looking classroom. I had posters and bulletin boards, student desks set up the way I wanted them, an excellent classroom library, and supplies for projects stored at the ready. This isn't bragging because most of the items in my classroom were purchased with tax payer dollars.

Each year, in my experience, teachers were given a specific sum that they could use to order supplies and equipment for their classroom. There were many differences between districts, not only in the amounts available to each teacher, but also in the methods used to purchase certain items. "Big ticket" items, such as student desks and chairs, were ordered by administrators.

Classroom Tales...

I worked in a district where teachers were expected to put together their order for the following year in January. I thought that was crazy for a lot of reasons. First, you've only gone through half of the school year, so you don't really know what you're going to need or want for the following year. Second, teachers change grade levels, curriculum changes, and teachers retire to be replaced by new teachers. Third, the number of sections in each grade level isn't known at this time so there isn't a complete understanding of needs for the following year. Finally, it's just too weird to be ordering in January for the following school year.

My first year as a principal, I encouraged teachers to be realistic in putting their orders together and aim for somewhere around $200-$250, but I don't believe I put an exact limit on their spending. One teacher submitted an order of $1,700. I learned my lesson and she learned that a small rural district doesn't have that kind of money.

My very first year of teaching, a colleague took me into the teacher's storeroom where supplies were kept for teachers to take as needs arose. I remember picking up a pack of pens or a roll of tape when he interrupted me and handed me a handful of the item. When I left that district twelve years later, there were still some items I hadn't run out of.

I would agonize for many hours as I went thought the catalogues and prioritized my needs. In the end, like most teachers, I spent every cent I was allowed and sometimes went over a little, hoping the principal wouldn't notice. By the way, also like most teachers, I hated it when told to figure 10% would be needed for shipping costs.

. . .

One district I worked in had two methods for ordering. One was to go through catalogues and find things you wanted to list on your regular order. The second was to look at a typed list of standard supplies that the district purchased in bulk, such as a particular pack of pencils, a certain model of stapler, etc. and order from that list. I made use of that list my first year until about half way through the school year when I asked for another of the three rolls of masking tape I had ordered and was told it was given to another teacher from the building supplies stockpile. From that moment on, I made sure never to order an item that was on that list of standard supplies.

... and Lessons Learned

Most of us like to know what's expected of us and what limitations there are. When it comes to ordering classroom supplies, it's just easier if teachers know how much they can spend.

When given the choice, many teachers would prefer to buy items locally because they can shop for the best deals, and then turn in the receipts to the business office. That sounds ideal, rather than ordering the same stapler for twice the price, but business people and auditors hate this.

Don't expect teachers to place orders for their classroom more than a few months in advance.

50

FIELD DAYS/TRACK MEET

After trying to teach 1st graders to do air high 5's and elbow bumps, some later complained that they were sore. One little girl remarked, "That's because they we're head bumping, belly bumping, and BOTTOM bumping each other!" When asked about this, they said, "Oh, yeah! Butt bumping is fun!"

There were always a lot of special activities that took place during the last few weeks of the school year. Everything was winding down, testing was over, and kids, as well as teachers, were looking forward to summer vacation.

Personally, I enjoyed the outdoor activities most of all, especially the field days or track meets planned by our gym teachers. Each of the schools I worked in had some kind of outdoor competition for the "older" elementary kids. The key word there is "competition" because, although those events were fun, there was definitely a competitive spirit between kids and teachers.

Classroom Tales…

It was the end of my first year as a classroom teacher and we were outside for the fifth grade track meet. I kept insisting that my students cheer for their classmates when I realized it was a waste of time to force them to be supportive. I just decided that I was going to cheer and they could do what they wanted. It was a good idea, but it would've been nice if I hadn't wasted the first hour nagging.

Some kids just ran inside to the bathroom every chance they got. I guess they weren't as excited as I was watching all of the races.

There was always at least one letter sent home about the day and what was expected in terms of dress, water, and sunscreen. I still remember one student wearing tall boots that she couldn't run in and another student who wore a heavy sweatshirt and jeans on a really hot day.

It probably wasn't a good idea, but I insisted that every kid put on sunscreen before going outside for the track meet. I brought in a pretty big container, which was shared by those who didn't bring their own.

One year a few kids ripped up their second place ribbons in anger after the events ended. That was a teachable moment for us all.

One of the students was running a longer race and was ready to give up. I ran with him on the outside of the track until he was close to the finish line. When he crossed that line, he got a lot of cheers. I, on the other hand, was just tired.

… and Lessons Learned

Forcing your students to cheer for anyone is a waste of time. They may follow that direction, but that's the only reason they'd be cheering. Instead, model the positive behavior that you want to see.

The same goes for sportsmanship. Trust me when I say that most teachers were competitive and wanted their classes to win but also knew that when it was over, everything was back to normal. Model that also.

Not all students will be into activities such as these. Some will be unhappy about having to participate in the first place, some are just not into the competitive aspects of the event, and some enjoy the day but aren't the star athletes. It's your job to help every student have a positive experience every school day, including this one.

51

CLASSROOM CONTROVERSIES

We're packing up our book bags at the end of the day and one kid didn't realize his bag wasn't zipped. So, as he starts walking everything falls out on the floor and he says, "Awww sh*t!"

For better or worse, the classroom has changed. Trust and respect between teacher and home has gone the way of the dinosaur in some ways, with there being no assumption that school personnel know what's best for kids. Whether it be related to assignments, class activities, books read, or interactions between teacher and students, everything that happens in school is called into question. Maybe I'm exaggerating. But, then again...

Classroom Tales...

One activity I did many years ago was related to the Revolutionary War and the advantages that the colonists had over the British when it came to "home field advantage". I used the example of Francis Marion, the "Swamp Fox", who fought the British in South Carolina and used the local landscape to evade the enemy. The activity went like this: I took my class down to the cafeteria where I had set up 6-8 garbage cans. I had my students get in a single line holding on to the person in front of them. First the line weaved through the cafeteria around the cans. Since they could see where they were going, it was easy, sort of like for Marion and his men, who knew the territory. Then, I had them do the same thing with their eyes closed. I watched them stumble around as they bumped into cans, like the British trying to catch Marion in unfamiliar territory. The activity went off without a hitch, took about 15 minutes, and students had fun while they learned. I describe this activity for a reason. Many problems could have occurred which would have been controversial. Kids touching garbage cans, having their hands on each other, bumping into cans when eyes were closed...these situations and others could have led to unhappy parents and lawsuits.

I also remember doing some role playing with students when teaching about slavery. Students took on the part of either slave or slave owner for a half day, which meant that the "slaves" had to get permission from their "owners" to do most anything, including using the bathroom, getting a drink, etc. At lunchtime, there was a "slave table" where the slaves had to sit and eat in silence. It's true that all participants volunteered and I sent home a letter to parents about this, but I felt that this activity was successful because students had at least a degree of understanding how dehumanizing slavery was. Could I use this activity in today's world?

A few years ago, a teacher was roundly criticized when she gave a writing assignment requiring students to "support" the Nazi position during World War Two.

.   .   .

I was speaking to my fifth graders when a student who had been out of the room came up behind me to join the class. I often moved my arms a lot when speaking, didn't see her, and smacked her in the face. She and her bloody nose went to the nurse. This happened approximately twenty-five years ago, but can you imagine what the reaction would be today? All many would hear is that a teacher struck a child in the face and she was injured. I would be crucified in the papers, on tv, and online, with many calls for me to be fired or prosecuted.

I read about a teacher who had students design posters depicting a slave auction, which were posted throughout the school.

Not too long ago, a high school teacher gave an assignment asking students to compare Donald Trump and Adolph Hitler.

... and Lessons Learned

Were these activities and/or events controversial? I believe so. Were the lessons poor choices? I suppose that depends on who you talk to. In some cases, I only know what I heard from others who were not part of the process. If students or parents were unhappy or offended, it is their right and obligation to share their concerns with the teacher, and if that didn't result in their concerns being met, they should have contacted the building administrator. Initially going to the local media or engaging in Facebook or Twitter rants won't address the problem because it's not a strategy to improve teaching and communication. It's simply a cowardly way of criticizing others.

My purpose here is twofold. First, to make clear the difficulties teachers face as they plan meaningful lessons for their students. Second, to recognize that there is an appropriate way for parents and students to address concerns, which begins with contacting the teacher directly, and the building principal if necessary.

Bluntly speaking, it's far easier to just stay in the classroom and teach from a textbook, but the best teachers are those that combine creativity and student involvement to provide experiences which kids will learn from and remember. Teachers should be encouraged to be creative in their lessons, but concerns must be voiced, as long as it's done with students in mind. After all, no child will remember work-book page 46.

As a teacher and also as a principal, I supported lessons which may have encouraged students to think "outside the box". However, like in the case of asking students to compare Trump and Hitler, you must keep your personal beliefs in check. As I wrote above, there may have been other factors and information I'm not aware of, but the teacher who assigned this topic may have stepped over the line.

52

MEETING NEXT YEAR'S TEACHER

On the first day of school, one little girl met her new teacher at the door and said hi. Then she walked across the hall to a different teacher and said, in a loud voice, "I was really hoping you were going to be my teacher this year."

Whether you are a student or a teacher, every new school year is, in a way, a "do over". The first step in that "do over" process was the first time students and "next year's teacher" got together. Impressions are made, good or bad, and you begin to look ahead to what you think the new year will be like.

Classroom Tales...

One year, when we didn't have a specific process in place when we would meet next year's class, I happened to be walking by the cafeteria when a teacher from 2nd grade asked if I wanted to meet the kids who would be with me in September. It seems they were sorting the kids in groups there.

· · ·

Some years when we did get a chance to meet next year's class, it was only for about ten minutes. I let them know I was not a "screamer", that we'd have fun, and I showed them a few things we'd be doing.

One fourth grader was suspended for the last few days of school and was in the main office when I walked by. He looked at me and told me how he hoped I'd be his teacher in fifth grade. I just told him I hoped so also, but the truth of the matter was that I knew when he was in third grade that he was coming my way.

One of the best decision I ever made, and I didn't do this until my last few years of my teaching career, was having my own "open house" a week or so before the school year began when my new students and parents could stop by, meet me, see the classroom, and leave school supplies if they wished. It worked like a charm while we got to at least put faces to names and I wished I had done that many years before.

A committee worked up a plan for students to meet their new teachers the last week of school. I thought they would arrange short visits in what would be their new classrooms. Instead, their idea was to have teachers stand in their doorways and wave to next year's class as they walked by.

… and Lessons Learned

If you have the chance to meet next year's class, they're probably going to be nervous about you as their teacher and have all sorts of thoughts about their new classmates. Help them to relax. There's no reason to share rules and expectations. Just make it a "meet and greet".

. . .

Kids want to meet their new teacher so find a way to get together before summer vacation. Even ten minutes would help everyone to relax as they head out for the summer. Encourage the building principal to arrange something.

Try not to take it personally if any of your future students share that they were hoping for a different teacher. I guess that's easier said than done, though.

53

THE END OF THE SCHOOL YEAR

"Thank you for teaching me to not be so annoying."

Towards the end of the school year, many teachers struggle with how to maintain the same rules, expectations, etc. as kids begin to concentrate more on summer vacation than on the work at hand. Of course, this is also true of teachers who look forward to the vacation as well.

In many schools, the last few weeks also see an uptick in special events, such as field trips and outdoor activities, which also lead to difficulties concentrating, not to mention the mix of half and full days in many schools.

Classroom Tales...

One of our last week activities one year was a water balloon fight. I know it's hard to believe, but I seemed to be under constant attack.

. . .

Most years we had a yearbook, either produced commercially or put together as a class activity, and had times that last week to sign each other's year books. I actually tried to write something personal, as did some students, while others wrote "have a great summer" in every book, and there was often a kid who would write a message to a classmate or me, but in the wrong yearbook.

As a fifth grade teacher in a K-5 school, we had an awards assembly. In addition to the official awards for academic excellence and physical education, we added several awards that were more personal for us in the way we viewed our students. The problem that developed was that we were directed to continue adding new awards until every student received one and you found, as a teacher, that it watered down the value of them. I remember one being something like "computer helper", which we used if we were desperate.

Ok, I admit it. I teared up when walking my students out for the last time most years.

When I joined one district as the elementary principal, I was almost immediately asked to change the graduation ceremony at the end of the year. It turned out that it had become this huge evening affair, with girls in gowns, boys in tuxes, and limos. Remember, that was an elementary school.

... and Lessons Learned

It can be difficult, but you must maintain your expectations right through to the very end of the school year, both for your students and yourself.

. . .

Beginning two to three months before the end of the school year, my kids would begin hearing how our school work wouldn't change until the final week. At that time we'd have fun, but not before. I did this so as to make the expectation clear that there was a lot of school and schoolwork left.

54

GETTING YOUR CLASSROOM READY FOR SUMMER

Since his teacher was always there when he got into the classroom and was always there when he left, he asked her one day, "Where do you keep your bed?"

It's a feeling unlike any other when you walk out of your classroom for the final time before summer vacation. There's excitement for the summer break, of course, but many teachers are already thinking about the next school year. I knew teachers that left their classroom all set up the way they wanted for the following year. In other words, they were all ready to go when they returned in the fall. Others, like me, just made sure to put things away, leave the room relatively neat, and take home things that I might need over the summer or were afraid would "disappear" if left in school.

Classroom Tales...

The key was that last week of school and enlisting student help. I was lucky, I think, because I taught kids old enough to help, but too young to complain about being "used".

I put up a list of things to do on the board that last week so my kids could see what had to be done and then they signed up with friends to do tasks they liked. My students were used to seeing lists and working off of them because I did similar things all year.

One of the items was always to label everything that wasn't bolted to the floor. The room would be emptied during the summer so the floor could be cleaned, so labeling had to be done so my stuff wouldn't disappear. My students knew that masking tape was their friend.

Some years, teachers were instructed to remove everything from the walls. I did this grudgingly, but others learned quicker than I did that it didn't really have to be done and they were much more ready for their new class in the fall.

I had a foolproof system that last day. The last thing I had to do was clear the top of my desk, which was where I put all of the things I didn't put away earlier in the week. I opened all of the drawers and pushed the remaining stuff in drawers until the following school year.

... and Lessons Learned

Label everything or risk losing things.

I didn't use movies often, but that last week was different. Have movies, games, etc. ready for the kids that have finished the things they agreed to do or are just not helping.

SUMMER

55

SCHOOL CALENDAR

One pet peeve someone shared was the frustration with lost instructional time because of events such as last minute assemblies. I'll add instructional time lost to meetings during the school day, whether it be grade levels, Committee on Special Education meetings, etc.

The school calendar for most schools has seen few changes over the years. Usually, there is a ten month school year surrounding a vacation in the summer, several vacations from a few days to a week and a half or so, and a variety of other days children have no school, whether it's for superintendent's conference days, one day holidays, etc. Parents, teachers, and kids have gotten used to this and I wouldn't want to be the person who decides that the school calendar needs an overhaul. That being said, the school calendar could use some tweaking.

Classroom Tales…

When I was a principal, there was a special breakfast for district faculty in the spring, which required a two hour delay. I was asked about three possible dates and I responded that I didn't care except to avoid the Friday before the three day Memorial Day weekend because many students wouldn't be in school that day if there was a two hour delay. Take a guess at the date chosen.

For the majority of my teaching years, my last day teaching was either the same day as students if they had a half day or I'd be required to come in the next morning for a few hours before heading home for the summer.

Because my wife and I were both teachers, we didn't take our kids out of school for vacations. We did go to Disney World once during a school vacation week. The crowds were disgusting- we actually went to attractions based on the length of the line, instead of whether we liked the attraction. I began to understand why parents take their kids out of school for vacations. Forget I said that.

… and Lessons Learned

If your district cares anything about the work done on Superintendent's Conference Days, they should NEVER schedule those days the day before school vacations. Like students, teachers are excited about the days off and not usually thinking about the topics presented.

Summer vacations are great for outdoor plans, family vacations, and so much more. However, if you want to avoid months of review in the fall, limit summer vacations to two months, maximum, not nine or ten weeks like it is in many schools. I actually think six to seven weeks would be better. Then again, I'm retired.

Teachers can't begin their contractual year a day or two before students and end their year the same day or the next day after kids go home for the summer. There is much to do and, just as important, it contributes to the idea that teachers work "part time". Even adding a week for teachers after kids go home for the summer and another week before the new school year begins would be a big step in the right direction. These weeks could be used for many purposes, including curriculum work, scheduling, etc.

There should seldom be a meeting that takes place during the school day that affects instructional time with kids. Schedule meetings before kids arrive or after they go home.

The official teacher day should be lengthened. Bear with me here. As I've stated elsewhere in this book, teachers want to, and should be, treated as professionals. Most teachers work at home and on the weekends now anyway, but nobody knows that. Also, if issues come up when kids arrive home from school parents may want to get in touch with a teacher as soon as possible if they have questions, etc. If teachers are in school, they can do their planning, correcting, etc., while still having time for these other tasks and contacting parents. Obviously, changes in the length of the school year or day would be addressed during negotiations, but I believe they are worth pursuing.

56

HOME SCHOOLING

You always found a way to keep me interested in what you were teaching.

S omeone recently told me that they were considering home schooling their children. There was no particular reason that led to this decision- they just thought it was something they wanted to do.

The perceptions that many public schools battle large class size, violence, and low test scores have been one factor that has led to more parents choosing to teach their children at home. Other parents want a focus on religious instruction or simply want to maintain a closer bond with their kids and believe home schooling will accomplish that.

Classroom Tales...

We held a dance in my elementary school one year and a parent contacted me, asking if their child who was being home schooled could attend. As Principal, I felt that social activities with other children her age would be good for the child and encouraged her to join us. There were definitely others who felt differently, that being home schooled meant that participating in school events should be off limits.

On the other hand, I was then asked by the same parent mentioned above if her niece, who was visiting the family, could also attend. I said no.

There were two children from one family who were Jehovah's Witnesses, one of whom I had in third grade. The student and his parents were great and we simply communicated often to make sure their religious beliefs were respected in terms of books read, celebrations, etc. I think they were pleased, but a year later both children were removed from our school so the parents could home school them.

More than once a parent was upset about something having to do with school and would then "threaten" that they were going to home school their child. I would always respond that whether to home school was certainly their right, but to make sure they understood what was involved and to make a well thought out decision.

... and Lessons Learned

Nothing is to be gained when school personnel and parents disagree to the point of hurting the child's educational program. As an administrator or teacher, do what's in the best interest of the student when it relates to a home schooled child.

. . .

Do what you can to understand why parents in your district choose to home school their children. Send out a survey or meet with parents. You, or they, might be surprised, and you both may end up improving the educational program for kids.

As a teacher you may find yourself with a student who had been home schooled before or may even be home schooled at the present time in the grade you're currently teaching. In the first case, you need to help that child adjust to a very different setting. In the second case, you may be called upon to "coordinate" between home and school. Regardless, be flexible and communicate openly.

57

BUILDING AND RENOVATION PROJECTS

Words no teacher wants to hear: "You taught my Daddy!"

In my thirty years in education, I went through two major renovation projects, as well as many smaller ones. I should say I "survived" two projects, as the additional stress that accompanies building or renovating a school takes a toll on everyone. Depending on the scope of the project, there are a variety of factors that affect the entire school community.

The planning phase can be enjoyable as new spaces are designed, furniture ordered, etc., but financial constraints and the difficulty in making decisions with so many stakeholder groups that will be affected can suck the joy right out of the process. If teachers and students are unlucky enough to have renovations or the construction of new spaces going on around them as they go about their business of teaching and learning, you can be assured of additional headaches regarding noise, dirt and construction debris, smells, etc. The real fun truly begins when the project is over. Just like in a home, there's nothing like new spaces and furnishings and, again, just like in a home, they won't look like new for very long.

Classroom Tales...

As the building principal, I still wore a jacket and tie, but my dress shoes were exchanged for Timberland shoes with a heavy sole I could wear while walking through construction debris each day.

We got to know the construction workers so well that we would ask about someone if we hadn't seen them during the day. One of our teachers even married one of the guys.

Fire drills became an adventure because we never knew which exits would be available when the alarm went off.

As principal, I would be asked to speak with the construction crew if workers were heard swearing or doing anything that seemed inappropriate on school grounds. One parent stopped in because she saw some of the guys at a local store buying beer and she thought they might be drinking on the job.

When I led my class through the halls, instead of the usual straight line, we would walk in more of a "snake" pattern to avoid rubble and building materials piled on the floor.

When I was in 4th grade, my school began building an addition for the new elementary school. I remember that the drilling and digging could be heard all throughout the day and the teachers hated it. Part of the construction included tearing down the playground, so at that point, recess consisted of playing in the school's parking lot. An odd choice if you ask me. The worst part of the construction? My class never was able to utilize the new building for which we had to suffer through all the construction because by the time the new elementary school was finished, we were in middle school.

I stayed in my office working as long as I could, but when the ceiling began falling around me during a phone call, it was time to leave. The good news is, I still have the orange hard hat I was given when construction began.

...and Lessons Learned

Sort of like in a marriage, working through a building or renovation project will add tension. Accept it and deal with it. Easy for me to say now.

The most effective strategy during the planning process is for all stakeholder groups to have input. For example, the art teacher should be involved in planning the art room, the music teacher the music room, etc.

That being said, everyone should understand upfront that there will be compromises. In other words, everyone has to be realistic in planning everything from the size of spaces to specific materials and furnishings.

If you're unfamiliar with OSHA regulations, that's going to change, especially if you're an administrator or head of a bargaining unit. By the way, I believe OSHA only addresses possible health issues for adults.

.   .   .

Visit other schools, especially those who've recently had renovations or new construction completed. Those visits provide design ideas, furniture choices, etc. That's what our librarian and art teacher did.

Depending on the ages of the children in the school under construction, find ways to involve students. It is a wonderful learning experience and it will show students that their opinions are valued. After all, we always say that schools are built for children.

58

EQUIPPING YOUR CLASSROOM WITH YOUR OWN MONEY

"I still remember the day you were teaching at the board when the marker wouldn't work and you threw it all the way across the room and we all laughed."

L ike most teachers I knew, I spent quite a bit of my own money on equipping and supplying my classroom. There was just so much money from the district to go around and most ordering had to be done at a deadline so I made many purchases during the school year as needs arose or items went on sale. Most educators did this and didn't receive, or expect, any funds in return, but I do believe that teachers simply wanted there to be an acknowledgement of our generosity. We wanted parents and students to know what we had done and hoped they were appreciative.

Classroom Tales...

Among the many books from home I brought in to my classroom was my collection of old "Peanuts" books I had from my childhood. Over time, they all disappeared except one, which I still have, but it's in pretty bad shape.

Each summer I would go to the Parent Teacher Store in Latham, NY to buy my plan book, literature units, bulletin board materials, stickers, and quite a few other things I hadn't been able to order or find before. I loved this visit, saw so many things for my classroom, and realized what a boring life I evidently led.

I bought a microwave for my classroom from a garage sale one spring. There were quite a few instances where I thought it would come in handy for projects, party items, etc. and was much more convenient than using the one in the faculty room myself or sending students down with a parent or other faculty member if I wasn't free. The very day I brought it in I received a memo stating that microwaves were no longer allowed in teacher's classrooms.

I don't like having garage sales at my house, but I enjoyed going to other people's garage sales because they were a great source for classroom materials. I had a terrific classroom library of several hundred books, the majority of which came from garage sales, as well as a pretty nice reading area, which was where students got to enjoy my big beanbag chair and my cane rocker, both garage sale items.

I mentioned above that I had a Bentley rocker with a cane seat. My students loved it for when they were reading silently, and often curled up in it with a friend. One day, one of my girls, who was quite small for third grade, was climbing up on it and her knee went through the seat. By the way, that little girl is now in a Doctoral program.

... and Lessons Learned

AC Moore and Staples were stores I frequented as a teacher, especially in the summer and around the holidays. They had great sales and helpful sales people.

When a local AC Moore was going out of business, I went there one last time, only to see mostly empty shelves and displays. I even took a photo.

When we set up our units and needed projects specific to a certain country, Oriental Trading was wonderful- cheap and simple.

59

PARENT AND TEACHER HANDBOOKS

A first grader had to give me a sentence with the word "shave". He said, "shave your back, maybe?" I asked who would do that. He said, "My dad because he is so hairy and his name is Hairy (Harry), too!

In some way, shape, or form, rules and procedures to follow are established and shared in some way, whether it be in a physical handbook, student agenda, or digitally. For teachers and other faculty members, conferences, attendance guidelines, etc. are shared with the expectations that they will be reviewed and kept as reference guides. Parents often receive theirs on the first day of school, when they are sent home with their child. Dress codes, academic requirements, attendance guidelines, homework expectations, and contact information may be included, as well, and a parent signature may be expected.

Classroom Tales...

I don't think I ever read the entire faculty handbook and I don't know any teacher who did. There were times, though, that we were asked to bring our copy to a faculty meeting and that led to a frantic search to find it.

Every once in a while, I'd contact a parent about one of the responsibilities listed in the handbook that either their child or they, themselves, weren't following.

By the end of the school year, most student agendas were worn out from daily use, but I did have a few students over the years whose agendas still looked fairly new. I'm not sure if this was good or bad.

... and Lessons Learned

The rule in my room was that if I forgot to have students record it in their agendas, they weren't responsible. This kept me on my toes.

There was a set time at the end of the day to record the homework assignments and notes in the agendas. Be careful, though, because there's always that student who gets called to go home fifteen minutes early.

Having the responsibilities for students, parents, and teachers listed in the same place meant that no one could claim ignorance about an expectation.

·   ·   ·

Have one student go around and check their classmate's agendas to make sure they're complete before kids leave.

60

TEACHER SALARIES AND TENURE

"I think you should go and play golf and take pictures of people and animals."

Numerous books and articles have been written on these topics because there are such differing opinions. I've worked in communities where teachers making $30,000 or more were considered overpaid. The thinking was, after all, they only worked "part time" and even then, they just taught kids like anyone could do. As for tenure- the guarantee of a job for life... just guess.

Classroom Tales...

I remember how excited my Mom was the first time I received tenure. I was a special education teacher, lowest on the list when it came to seniority, but Mom thought that having tenure meant I'd automatically have a job forever.

· · ·

When I was a new principal, I was at a workshop with other administrators and teachers when the topic of tenure came up. Teachers
there stated that if a principal did their job in supervising the first
three years of a new teacher's career, there would be no concerns
about tenure. They felt those first three years were long enough to get
rid of incompetent teachers.

When the negotiating teams representing the teachers and the
district exchanged initial proposals, the district proposed a zero
percent increase and the union proposed something in the neighborhood of eighteen percent. I was told that this was typical and was
viewed as a starting point. It seemed like a huge waste of time to me,
but I didn't say that out loud.

A speech teacher I know walked away from teaching after approximately twelve to fifteen years. None of us could understand how he
could give up the guarantee of tenure and his future pension.

I had never been evaluated when I received tenure for the first time.

I worked with a teacher who was one of the first to arrive in the
morning and the last to leave after school, even after teaching for
over twenty-five years. I also worked with a teacher that was still
teaching after twenty five years because, although the school district
she was employed by felt she was very ineffective, her supervisors
were unwilling to pursue the very lengthy and costly process involved
in removing her.

… and Lessons Learned

Having been both a teacher and an administrator has given me a broader view of tenure. I've worked with wonderful teachers, some new to the field and also veterans with ten, twenty, or thirty years or more of experience. I've also worked with teachers who should never have entered the field of education in the first place or, at the least, should not have remained.

How many times have you, or will you, hear about teaching because you love kids and not for the money?

Not everyone should be a teacher, I think we can all agree on that. But that guarantee of a job that is part of tenure, along with the benefits that come with it, make it very difficult to walk away once you're hired.

61

RETENTION

"When I heard I was going to be in third grade again I was sad. But when I came into your class, I knew I was going to have a great time."

"**B**ack in the day", we used the terms "failed" or "kept back" to describe a student who was retained. I don't think that perception has changed that much from students and even parents. There are two clear trains of thought here. First, if a student hasn't mastered the material from a grade level and shows no sign that he/she will be successful in the next grade, why should the child move on? Second, there is little educational research to suggest that retention works. That child who is retained may never master the material in a grade, whether it be a second year or more. What then? The process starts with why that student is being retained and why it will be successful. Is it academic, social, emotional, or something else entirely? By the way, what if there is a disagreement between teacher, principal, or parent? Who makes the final decision?

Classroom Tales...

When I was teaching fifth grade, I once had twin boys who had always been in the same class. We ended up retaining one of them. That wasn't easy for anyone, especially the brother who was retained.

A principal once told me that if a parent was against their child being retained, they would make certain that the retention was unsuccessful.

One third grader told me that when she found out that I would be her teacher for her second year in third grade she knew it would be a good year. Talk about pressure!

... and Lessons Learned

I believe that the final decision regarding a student being retained should be made by school personnel, although everything should be done to get parents on board.

It makes absolute sense that a child shouldn't go on to the next grade unless they're ready academically, socially, etc. However, there is no research that I know of that supports retention. The decision to retain is often based on emotion and frustration.

If you're going to retain a child, at least make sure it's in the early grades because, in general, there is less of a stigma attached.

62

CHOOSING CURRICULUM MATERIALS

I put up a picture of Mount Rushmore and one little girl says, "I know what that is! It's the wall the president is building!"

The easiest way to teach is to have your students get out the appropriate textbook or workbook and continue from the day before. However, there are problems with this approach, beginning with how to choose the materials you're going to use in your classroom. As a new teacher, your job is to use what you're given if there is a specific series for a specific subject.

Classroom Tales...

I once served on a district committee tasked with choosing a social studies series to be used in the three elementary schools. We had presentations from publishers and piloted the final choices in all three schools with input before choosing the one that was considered the best. A year later, I was told that the teachers in one building never used the series and the new materials were still in boxes.

. . .

A third grade teacher once told me that her students knew there were fifty states even though the United States map on her wall only had forty eight states.

I remembered using a couple of series over the years that we called "vegetarian" because there was no meat to them.

I worked with a librarian once who felt it was her responsibility to read every book before making it available to students. A noble effort, but she had ten unopened boxes of new books on her shelves because she hadn't had a chance to read them.

The best two series I worked with were the Voyagers reading program and the Saxon math program. Neither one was what you would call "pretty", but both were challenging and effective. By the way, I was unhappy with both when they were ordered.

... and Lessons Learned

Get those who will be using the materials involved in choosing the materials. You have a better chance of more effective purchases and it encourages ownership.

Look at more than the initial cost. Are some of the materials disposable so they have to be purchased each year? Are there lots of copies to be made each week and, if so, who will be making them?

63

EDUCATORS IN CHARGE OF SCHOOLS

An administrator was negotiating with the district and the rumor was that it didn't go well for him. One sweet little third grader explained it this way: "Mr. M just got the shaft!"

When I was a kid, there was no doubt that teachers were in charge of the classrooms because that's who gave me my grades and sent notes home or made phone calls. Principals were the real bosses in school although I don't remember having much contact with them, other then when I broke auditorium seats with a piano...and when I knocked over a row of typewriters when wrestling. As to superintendents and school boards, I don't remember them at all.

If we fast forward to the last five to ten years, I don't know if school personnel are in charge anymore. For a variety of reasons, roles have changed with teachers, administrators, and school boards being challenged for what seems to be every action they take. Every district I know has lawyers on retainer. Parents and/or their children struggle for control over everything from dress codes and playground rules to field trip choices and what books are read aloud. Government involvement at all levels extends into the classroom, not only in regards to standardized testing, but also daily curriculum, teacher evaluation, the content of textbooks, etc. Who is in control of our schools? Who should be?

Classroom Tales...

A colleague of mine had a student whose parent sent her a seating chart detailing the desks arrangement and where each child in the class should sit. The note, which I read, wasn't simply offering a suggestion- it was more of a "directive".

I had a rule in my class that if a student did poorly on a spelling test, I would have them practice their words for five minutes at the start of recess. One parent complained to the principal about this so we had a meeting. The parent suggested that her son write the words that were missed ten times each for homework, each night during the week, until the next test. That idea came from the parent and I agreed, while stating it was more work than practicing the words with a friend.

During the last few years I was in the classroom, more and more standardized testing was added to the elementary grades. Students obviously didn't want them and many teachers didn't see the need or believe in the value of them. Lawmakers and companies that produced these tests supported them, and one result was that additional testing was accompanied by additional spending on test preparation materials.

... and Lessons Learned

In every possible way, including in a parent/teacher handbook, letters sent home, and in the way every day questions or issues are addressed, it must be made clear that teachers are in charge of their classrooms and the principal is in charge of the school.

This is difficult, but, although different levels of government may be involved in setting up school curriculum guidelines, school personnel must decide on the materials used and how the instruction is delivered to students.

I think that one of the reasons there are questions about who's in charge of schools is because of all the criticism that is heaped on teachers, public schools, teacher unions, etc. As a woman I used to work with liked to say- Schools need to man up! Educators at all levels need to take back their authority.

Parents and others in the school community will respect school decisions more when they know their feelings and concerns are being addressed. There are many ways to do this, but simple courtesy and respect work best, along with a healthy dose of common sense. Regardless, although compromise is a wonderful tool to use with parents in some situations, it must still be made clear that the final decision is up to educational professionals.

End certain practices that cede classroom control to others, such as parental requests for their child's teachers. Also, make it clear that the same courtesy and respect that educators should practice should also be expected from parents, school board members, etc.

64

THE FACULTY ROOM

"My grandmother says she had you for third grade. I knew you were old, but I didn't think you were that old!"

Every elementary school that I know has a faculty room- a designated space for teachers to eat lunch in, share stories from their day, or possibly to just take a break. It's also a good place for complaining about whatever's on your mind.

Classroom Tales...

Each month, the teachers in one grade were responsible for bringing in a snack for faculty members to enjoy in the morning and/or throughout the day. It could be anything from chips and dip to brownies. After a while of this, we stopped because everyone was gaining weight.

.   .   .

I was subbing at a school and ate lunch in the faculty room several times. No one who worked there ever said a word to me.

Students weren't really allowed in the faculty room, but when one kid came in to get something out of the refrigerator, the conversation immediately changed.

An apartment mate of mine liked to bake and made bagels once. They were good, but he left them out overnight and they were like rocks in the morning. I brought them to my school's faculty room and every single one was eaten by the end of the day.

I was eating lunch in the faculty room when I found a long hair in the sandwich I was eating. I tried to pull it out, hoping no one noticed what I was doing.

In the district I was working in, the faculty room in one school was only for teachers. No one else in any other position was allowed in there.

... and Lessons Learned

Eating lunch or just taking a short break in the faculty room is a nice opportunity to get to know colleagues. It's also nice to get away from your classroom for a bit.

Be part of making your faculty room a warm and inviting place for subs, all staff members, and even visitors from other schools. That kindness not only helps everyone to do a better job, it adds to projecting a positive image.

65

FACULTY AND COMMITTEE MEETINGS

When a teacher shares that she was going to have a knee replacement, a student comments "Oh, my grandma had one of those."

I can't think of one person in any profession that looks forward to sitting in meetings. Teachers aren't any different.

Classroom Tales...

A superintendent I know always encouraged new teachers to join committees their first year. PLEASE DON'T! You have enough to do and learn when you start out. Give yourself time to breathe before you take on anything else. By the way, my wife, also a retired teacher, feels the opposite way.

I remember a teacher who always brought papers to correct or planning to do when she attended a faculty meeting.

. . .

I worked with an administrator who always began his meetings at least ten to fifteen minutes later than scheduled. Soon, we began arriving ten to fifteen minutes after the expected start time.

A principal I worked with conducted faculty meetings that lasted eight to ten minutes. I'm sure she thought teachers would like her because of it and she was probably right.

I once had teacher union officers remind me that I had to cancel that day's faculty meeting because their contract stated that a faculty meeting on Monday couldn't occur after a three day weekend- we had a snow day on the previous Friday. They were right.

...and Lessons Learned

If you're a principal or committee chair- really anyone who's responsible for running a meeting- cancel one once in a while. You'll be really popular, at least for a few minutes.

Don't have a meeting just because you're supposed to. If there aren't any issues to discuss, don't meet.

If you're in charge of a meeting, start your meeting on time, have a clear, realistic agenda, and end the meeting as quickly as your agenda is covered. Most everyone has other things to do.

66

PARENT/TEACHER ORGANIZATIONS

A little boy came in and told all of us how his family bought a "cheap parakeet" the night before. As it turns out, the family bought a Jeep Cherokee.

PTA has been around forever it seems. As kids, our parents joined PTA, took part in bake sales and volunteered on committees. Some parents even became "room parents", helping the teacher with classroom chores. In many school districts, the role of the local parent teacher organization hasn't changed in the work they do for schools. That's too bad because the role that parents play in their child's education has evolved in several ways and the coordination of parental efforts can help to improve the educational program.

Classroom Tales...

Somewhere around my house I have a PTA pin that was given to me signifying lifetime membership. I thought it was impressive until I was told I would still have to renew my membership and pay dues each year.

I was the teacher representative for our school's PTA at a time when the relationship between teachers and the community was very negative. With one hundred percent teacher membership being the goal, it took quite a bit of encouraging. I always thought some teachers joined because they felt sorry for me being the teacher rep, and I remember reaching our goal when the art teacher agreed to join just to help me out.

Our PTA organized monthly activities for both students and their families. We held everything from roller skating to family dances to movie nights. This was especially important in a rural district with little for the kids to do outside limited sports.

At a statewide PTA conference I listened as speakers described the need for teachers to be better role models. A parent interrupted the speaker to call a "point of order", or whatever part of Robert's Rules allowed for an immediate interruption, to complain that someone had stolen bottles of liquor from her room.

Each school year, the PTA would organize special events to show appreciation for their school's teachers. This could be anything from a picnic to treats brought in to the faculty room to a catered luncheon. All were greatly appreciated by most!

...and Lessons Learned

PTA, PTO PTSO (Parent-Teacher-Student Organization)... It really doesn't matter what its called as long as it builds on the positive foundation of a school. There is so much that a parent teacher group can do to be a part of a school, as long as it is viewed as a partner, not as a threat.

As much as I believe that a PTA group can, and should, be involved in more "in depth" school issues, traditional activities such as fundraising are welcomed, also. I've seen and appreciated parents volunteering at everything from running book fairs to school picture day. Many of these efforts began with a request to the school parent teacher organization.

Presentations on classroom projects and student activities at PTA meetings go a long way to establish PTA as the official parent group in a school. If kids attend and contribute, it's even better.

In a district I worked in PTA was asked to appoint one or more people to be on an interview committee. This served several purposes. First, it built on the image of PTA as an official school partner. Second, PTA lived up to this image and was more responsive in it's participation. Third, PTA was selective in choosing representatives, where as if certain parents were chosen by the principal or teachers, it could be viewed as favoritism or some kind of token step to involve parents.

67

VISITOR POLICIES AND SCHOOL SAFETY

This was shared by a "specials" teacher (art, gym, music, library). "Fire drills almost always happen at the same time during the day and affect the same grade."

Most of us assume that a school, especially an elementary school, will be a welcoming environment. As having been both a principal and a teacher, I loved visitors and students knew this. I suppose it was a sign of pride for me that we had visitors from other schools and school districts. In addition to students, many parents and area residents visited for conferences, performances, etc.

In this day and age, for a variety of reasons, most schools have instituted policies to ensure the safety of all those who attend school by identifying every individual who enters the building. When I sub now, for example, I have to be buzzed in by school personnel. It's a sign of the times.

Classroom Tales...

When I was a teacher "back in the day", our doors were never locked. One day, two men walked in the front door, through the hallways, and out the back door. They didn't do anything and didn't even talk to anybody. We realized then that we had to establish some guidelines for visitors.

We had badges for visitors and volunteers. The badges were the brightest/ugliest colors you can imagine, orange and green if I remember, and it seemed you could see them for miles! That, of course, was the point.

When my district was in the planning stages for a major construction project, I toured a relatively new elementary school in hopes of getting design ideas. As I walked in the front door, I saw a beautiful lobby with high, arching ceilings, and stairs leading to second floor classrooms. The problem was that there was no one near the entry-way, with the main office being approximately fifty feet away and through a door. Anyone could enter the building and go to any location in the school, including classrooms, without being seen, welcomed, or checked in.

One morning a mom showed up and wanted to see her kids, but couldn't because there was a custody agreement in place and she had no visitation rights. She went through most of a box of tissues while she cried in my office begging me.

Parents in one elementary school entered their children's classrooms during the school day whenever they wished to talk to teachers.

. . .

In mid January, we implemented new visitor procedures that restricted parents from walking their child to the classroom. Before this change, quite a few, especially in kindergarten, would stay and help their child with their coat, lunch, and getting settled in. One mom, when saying good bye to her kindergartener, pointed at me and explained to the child that "the man" wouldn't let her walk down to the classroom anymore and help.

Even after we had policies about locking doors, school personnel would place a wooden wedge or a chair in the doorway so they wouldn't be locked out if they went to their car or were going out on the playground and didn't have their key.

I'm not much of a rebel, but I have to admit that I went years without wearing my teacher id badge and I was never asked about it.

...and Lessons Learned

Be proactive. Don't wait for an incident to occur before you establish guidelines for visitors. The bottom line is that there should never be a person who enters the building without having been identified by those school personnel responsible for this task.

I like the badge system, but like any new rule at school, home, or in the workplace, it must be enforced consistently. Our students knew of this policy and would say something to their teacher if they saw someone they didn't know without a badge.

Speaking of badges, our rule was that ANYONE who didn't work in OUR school had to wear one. This included parents, teachers, and administrators from other schools in our district, but also the superintendent and Board of Education members- this was not always well received!

Like with any new procedures, make sure to involve those directly affected with the development or revisions. We had a short term committee that put visitor policies together, then presented this plan to our PTA and the school board (in both cases, with prior notice that discussion would take place), before notifying parents what the new policies were and when they would be in effect.

AUTHOR'S NOTE

It's my hope that those who've read *The Real Classroom* will have a much clearer idea of what's really involved with teaching and attending school. I believe that teaching our children and helping them to grow as individuals is as important as any task that's part of any profession. I've been fortunate to not only have been a teacher, but also a school administrator and a parent. I've spent my entire life surrounded with kids and I wouldn't have it any other way!

If you wouldn't mind, I'd appreciate it if you'd consider doing two things:

First, please leave a review of *The Real Classroom* on your favorite book buying website.

Second, please visit my website and join my email list at www. jimsack.com. You'll receive a free gift, and occasional emails concerning upcoming books of mine, such as the newest book in my *Oh, No!* series, as well as special offers and news of my FREE visits to schools, libraries, etc.

Thanks for reading *The Real Classroom* and for your time!

Jim

Ordering Information:

Special discounts are available on quantity purchases by school districts, educators, associations, and others. For details, please contact the author at www.jimsack.com or by email at jim@jimsack.com

Made in the USA
Middletown, DE
08 December 2020